Programming Investment in the Process Industries
An Approach to Sectoral Planning

M.I.T. MONOGRAPHS IN ECONOMICS

Programming Investment in the Process Industries

An Approach to Sectoral Planning

DAVID A. KENDRICK

THE M.I.T. PRESS

Massachusetts Institute of Technology
Cambridge, Massachusetts, and London, England

To My Parents

Preface

The rapid pace of development of electronic computers has provided the economist and economic planner with powerful tools that have not yet been fully exploited. Present methods of project analysis for investment planning offer a striking example of this discrepancy. In both private industrial firms and in government planning organizations analysts still calculate rates of return for individual projects without taking into consideration the strong interdependencies that may exist between projects and/or the desirability of scheduling them over time in a complementary fashion. This procedure has been followed because of the magnitude of the calculations involved in considering all the possible combinations of projects in an interrelated system.

The widespread availability of computers now permits the analyst to construct models for sectors of economic systems and to use these models to study interdependent investment projects. The planner for the private firm is thus provided with a method of studying the effects of investments in his own firm on his competitors and vice versa. In a similar manner the government planner obtains an approach for evaluating the claims of different plants for funds with which to expand their capacity.

This study describes a computable model that has been devised for analyzing groups of interdependent investment projects in the process industries. In Part I the equations of the model are developed and written out. Then, since the separation between writing down the equations for a model and the preparation of the model for solution on a computer is often great, Part II is devoted to a detailed description of the method used in setting up the model for solution of an investment planning problem in the Brazilian steel industry.

I should like to express my appreciation to the persons and organizations who assisted me in the completion of this study. Richard Eckaus, Charles Kindleberger, and Robert Solow provided many helpful suggestions and comments in the development of my doctoral dissertation on which this volume is based. The class of investment problems to which this research has been directed was brought to my attention by Paul N. Rosenstein-Rodan. Louis Lefeber and Thomas Vietorisz gave generously of their time and assistance in the early phases of this study. Richard Eckaus, Michael Bruno, Martin Weingartner, Stephen Marglin, and particularly Alan Manne made comments on my thesis that were most helpful in the rewriting of it for this volume. Henry Jacoby and George Waardenberg offered the kind of continuing discussion, criticisms, and references that only fellow students can provide.

The Brookings Institution provided financial support during the development of the thesis with a grant under their Transportation Research Program, and Alan Abouchar of that Institution helped by reading the material that is now in Chapters 4 and 5. The Center for International Studies at the Massachusetts Institute of Technology provided financial help and a stimulating atmosphere in which to work during the rewriting of the thesis. Project MAC and the Computation Center at the Massachusetts Institute of Technology permitted the use of their computational facilities.

I owe a special debt to the officials of the major steel companies of Latin America and to the officials of the government and private organizations which work with this industry. Their hospitality, openness, and patience in teaching have contributed greatly to this study.

Finally, to my wife Gail for her continuing help goes my immeasurable gratitude.

DAVID A. KENDRICK

Cambridge, Mass.
August 1966

Contents

ix

Tables

Figures

1

Introduction

Although the art of project analysis for investment decisions has developed rapidly in the last fifty years, it is only with the advent of the electronic computer that interdependencies between projects have become an integral part of the analyses. Traditionally, a rate of return or present value has been calculated for each project, the projects ranked, and those projects that fall within the budget constraint have been chosen for execution. The fact that two or more of the projects might be interdependent was alluded to as having an effect on the rate of return or present value, and mention was made that these interdependencies could be taken into account by combining the projects and calculating a rate of return or present value on the combined project. However, this sort of analysis was rarely if ever carried out because of the extent of the calculations involved in repeating the operation once for each possible combination of interdependent projects.

For some industries the assumption of independence of investment projects may not be damaging to the analysis. In others it may be very important. In the process industries the interdependencies between investment projects in a single plant are strong because the product flows from one productive unit to another in a series of processes. A bottleneck at any one facility will have substantial effects on the profitability of investments in nearby productive units. In a similar fashion, increases in capacity in one plant may have a large impact on the expected rate of return from investments to increase capacity in other plants within the same region.

The purpose of the investigation discussed in these pages was to develop an investment planning model for the process industries and to apply that model to an investment problem in the steel industry in Brazil.

Our focus is on the following type of investment planning problem:

A planner who is employed by a business firm or by a government agency and who is responsible for investment analysis in a single industrial sector for a region, a country, or a common market area sends out to the plants projections of the requirements for the industry's products in the market areas of the region during the coming decade. In due course he receives from the companies feasibility studies on a group of investment projects, some of which are for additions to capacity in existing facilities and others for the establishment of new plants. The planner must then choose from among the projects and schedule them over time in such a way as to minimize the total investment, production, and transportation cost in the industry while continually fulfilling the evolving market requirements.

Our approach to this problem is to build a mathematical model of the industry that can be used to study the effects on the industry of various combinations of investments and of different schedules of investment projects over time. For example, let us assume that two steel plants owned by the same company both submit projects to the investment planner for the installation of new tinning lines. The two plants are located near enough to one another for a part of their market areas to overlap. The investment planner is then faced with the decision of whether or not the projects should be executed and of scheduling them over time so as to take the maximum advantage of the interdependencies. With a mathematical model of the industry the planner can study the effects on the industry of various combinations of the investments in space and time. In the model he may try installing one of them immediately and the other four years hence, both of them immediately, one next year and one three years later, and in any other combinations that may seem promising.

Doubtless many business firms or government planning offices go through this type of operation of considering various combinations of investments and schedulings of investments. The model developed in this volume provides simply a means of increasing the efficiency of this process by setting down all the calculations in such a form that they can be performed on an electronic computer. Moreover, the results of the study show that by constructing models of a certain form it is possible to rule out some combinations of investments as so relatively undesirable that the calculations need not be made for them.

We begin by constructing a linear programming[1] model which de-

---

[1] For the reader who is not familiar with mathematical programming, an effort has been made to explain each concept as it appears. For example, in the following sections diagrams are used to explain the model concurrently with the writing down of the equations. However, no comprehensive attempt is made in this study to explain mathematical programming. Any number of books on the subject are widely available. See, for example, Saul I. Gass, *Linear Programming,*

scribes the industry and the markets in a region at time zero, that is, at the time that the investment planner is making his decisions. This model, which is developed in Chapter 2, includes estimates of (1) the product requirements for each of the industry's products in all of the market areas, (2) the capacity of all major productive units in each plant in the region, (3) the cost of producing each of the products in every plant, (4) the cost of transporting the products from the plants to the market areas, (5) the cost of importing the products to the market areas, (6) expected profits on exports, and (7) the cost of shipping intermediate products between plants. This single-period model is a useful instrument for studying the operation of the existing system but is insufficient for analyzing investment problems. Therefore, in Chapter 3 the model is converted to a multiperiod model and investment decision variables are added.

Since there is a wide gap between writing down the equations for an industrial model and the application of such a model to an actual investment planning problem, Chapters 4 through 7 are devoted to a description of the use of the models on a problem in the Brazilian steel industry. The single-period model is presented first along with a discussion of a detailed sensitivity analysis that was made to examine the effect of changes in product requirements and in the costs of production and transportation. Then a description is given of the application of the multiperiod model to the problem of when and where to add to productive capacity in a system of three steel mills and three market areas.

Methods and Applications (New York: McGraw-Hill Book Company, 1958), or G. Hadley, *Linear Programming* (Reading, Mass.: Addison-Wesley Publishing Co., Inc., 1962).

PART I

Development of the Model

The Single-Period Model

As mentioned earlier, our objective here is to construct a small mathematical model to describe the condition of the industry at the time that the investment planner is making his decisions. Whether the model is to be used by a private business or by a government planning agency, it is desirable to include all of the production facilities in the region and not just those that belong to the company or organization making the study. The reason for this is that the private businessman will want to study the impact of his competitors' investments on his business and vice versa, and the government planner will want to take advantage of the complementarities of investments between plants as well as within plants.

We begin with a distribution of production facilities in a region and a distribution of the markets that consume the products of the industry. For example, let P_1, P_2, and P_3 in Figure 2.1 represent three plants and M_1, M_2, and M_3 represent cities that constitute the principal market areas for the products of the industry. The arrows then represent shipments of products from the plants to the markets.

Let us first assume that the industry produces only a single commodity and that each of the plants can produce only up to a certain fixed amount of the product. Furthermore, we assume that each market area will consume a certain fixed amount of the product no matter what the price may be. This assumption will be adequate for most industries if the price changes are very small and for some industries even if the price changes are very large. This, of course, depends on many factors, among which one of the most important is the availability of substitutes for the products and the prices of these substitutes. In some process industries the principal products are used as intermediate products by other industries in producing goods that are purchased by the consumer. For these industries the effect of price changes will depend, among other

7

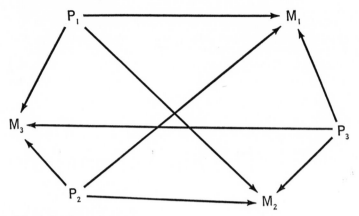

FIGURE 2.1. *A simple spatial model.*

things, on whether or not other materials can be substituted for those produced by the industry.

We represent the capacity of the ith plant with γ_i and the consumption requirements of the jth market area by σ_j where the units of each of these parameters are so many physical units per year of the product. Furthermore, we let w_{ij} denote the amount of the commodity produced at plant i and shipped to market area j, and we let c_{ij} represent the cost of producing a unit of the product in plant i and shipping it to market area j. Then the total cost of production and transportation may be written

$$Z = \sum_i \sum_j c_{ij} w_{ij}. \tag{2.1}$$

We desire to minimize this cost while at the same time fulfilling the product requirements of the market areas; that is, the amount of product shipped from all of the plants to each market area must be at least as great as the requirements. We write this as

$$\sum_i w_{ij} \geq \sigma_j, \quad \text{all } j. \tag{2.2}$$

Thus the requirements at each of the $j = 1, 2, \cdots, m$ market areas must be fulfilled.

Furthermore, each plant cannot produce more than its capacity, so we write

$$\sum_j w_{ij} \leq \gamma_i, \quad \text{all } i; \tag{2.3}$$

that is, the total of the shipments from plant i to all of the market areas must be less than or equal to the capacity of the ith plant.

We assume for the moment that the total capacity available in all of the plants is equal to the total product requirement in all of the markets; that is,

$$\sum_i \gamma_i = \sum_j \sigma_j. \tag{2.4}$$

This assumption will be dropped in the next section.

Finally, we constrain all the variables to be greater than or equal to zero; that is, it is impossible to ship a negative amount of goods from a plant to a market. We write these constraints as

$$w_{ij} \geq 0, \quad \text{all } i, j. \tag{2.5}$$

Then, if we take the example of the industry shown in Figure 2.1 with three plants and three market areas, our mathematical model of the industry may be written as

$$\text{Minimize } Z = c_{11}w_{11} + c_{12}w_{12} + c_{13}w_{13} + c_{21}w_{21} + \cdots + c_{33}w_{33} \tag{2.6}$$

subject to

$$\begin{aligned}
w_{11} + w_{21} + w_{31} &\geq \sigma_1, \\
w_{12} + w_{22} + w_{32} &\geq \sigma_2, \\
w_{13} + w_{23} + w_{33} &\geq \sigma_3;
\end{aligned} \tag{2.7}$$

$$\begin{aligned}
w_{11} + w_{12} + w_{13} &\leq \gamma_1, \\
w_{21} + w_{22} + w_{23} &\leq \gamma_2, \\
w_{31} + w_{32} + w_{33} &\leq \gamma_3;
\end{aligned} \tag{2.8}$$

$$\gamma_1 + \gamma_2 + \gamma_3 = \sigma_1 + \sigma_2 + \sigma_3; \tag{2.9}$$

$$w_{11}, w_{12}, w_{13}, w_{21}, w_{22}, w_{23}, w_{31}, w_{32}, w_{33} \geq 0. \tag{2.10}$$

This type of model is called a linear programming transportation model and can be solved with computer codes designed specifically for this class of problems.[1]

The solution of the model would tell us that, given a certain geographic distribution of production capacity and of market requirements and a knowledge of the costs of production and transportation in the system, we could determine how much should be produced at each factory for shipment to each market area.

Although the model is easy to solve, it is much too simple for our

---

[1] The linear programming transportation problem was originally formulated by R. L. Hitchcock in "Distribution of a Product from Several Sources to Numerous Localities," *Journal of Mathematical Physics,* Vol. 20 (1941), and was clarified and solved by T. C. Koopmans in "Optimum Utilization of the Transportation System," *Econometrica,* Vol. 17, Supplement (1949). The production-transportation variant of this classic problem is discussed in G. Hadley, *Linear Programming* (Reading, Mass.: Addison-Wesley Publishing Co., Inc., 1962), pp. 431–433.

purposes. Thus, we proceed by making a series of modifications to this mathematical model in an attempt to make a more accurate portrayal of the industry while at the same time keeping the model simple enough for us to solve. We do this by adding (1) multiple products, (2) shipments of intermediate products between plants, (3) imports, and (4) exports.

Multiple Products

We introduce multiple products by assuming that the industry produces $k = 1, \cdots, \kappa$ intermediate products and $k = \kappa + 1, \cdots, K$ final products in $e = 1, 2, \cdots, E$ productive units at each plant. We denote the amount of capacity required in productive unit e at plant i to produce a unit of product k with the coefficient α_i^{ke}. Since each product receives a different degree of processing, most products do not pass through all the productive units in which cases $\alpha^{ek}_i = 0$ for those units.

Figure 2.2 gives an example of multiple products in a process industry manufacturing facility. At each stage in the manufacturing line a product may be passed on to the next productive unit or it may be sent out of

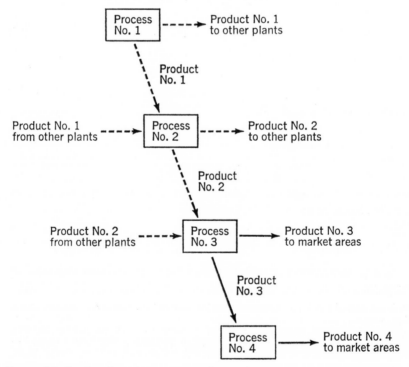

FIGURE 2.2. *Product flows in a process industry plant.*

the plant as intermediate product[2] to be used by another plant in the same industry or as a final product to be used by consumers or by a plant in another industry. The amount of product that can pass through any process is limited by the capacity of the productive unit for that process. However, capacity bottlenecks may be broken or bypassed by bringing in intermediate products from other plants.

In the example shown in Figure 2.2 the number of productive units is $E = 4$, the number of intermediate products is $\kappa = 2$, and the total number of products (both intermediate and final) is $K = 4$. The coefficient α_1^{23} then represents the amount of capacity in the first plant and in the third productive unit of that plant which is required to produce each unit of product number two.

With multiple products and productive units in the model we denote the requirements for product k in market area j by σ_j^k, and the capacity of productive unit e in plant i by γ_i^e. Therefore our model becomes

Objective Function:

$$\text{Minimize } Z = \sum_i \sum_j \sum_{k=\kappa+1}^{K} c_{ij}^k w_{ij}^k \qquad (2.11)$$

subject to capacity utilization constraints,

$$\sum_j \sum_{k=\kappa+1}^{K} \alpha_i^{ke} w_{ij}^k \leq \gamma_i^e \qquad \text{all } i, e, \qquad (2.12)$$

market requirement constraints,

$$\sum_i w_{ij}^k \geq \sigma_j^k \qquad \text{all } j; k = \kappa + 1, \cdots, K, \qquad (2.13)$$

nonnegativity constraints,

$$w_{ij}^k \geq 0 \qquad \text{all } i, j; k = \kappa + 1, \cdots, K. \qquad (2.14)$$

We have now dropped the constraints that total productive capacity must equal total product requirement in the system. The model thereby loses its special character as a transportation problem and becomes an ordinary linear programming problem.

Interplant Shipments of Intermediate Products

As was shown in Figure 2.2, the effects of capacity bottlenecks can be mitigated and underutilization of capacity decreased by means of shipment of intermediate products between plants. In industries where there

---

[2] We use the terms intermediate and final products in reference to the industry being studied. Thus any product sent out of the industry, whether to a consumer or to another industry, is a final product, and any product sent to another plant in the same industry is an intermediate product.

are large economies of scale or indivisibilities these activities may be very important.[3]

Therefore, we add to our model activities that we denote by u_{il}^k for shipments of intermediate product k from plant i to plant l. Then we add the term

$$\sum_i \sum_{i \neq l} \sum_{k=1}^K a_{il}^k u_{il}^k \qquad (2.15)$$

to the objective function to account for the additional production and transportation cost in the system.[4]

The addition of these activities for shipments of intermediate products between plants has no effect on the market requirement constraints as they only constrain the model to provide sufficient *final* goods. The capacity constraints are affected, however, by these additional variables through the addition of the following terms:

$$\sum_{l \neq i} \sum_{k=1}^K \alpha_i^{ke} u_{il}^k - \sum_{l \neq i} \sum_{k=1}^K \alpha_l^{ke} u_{li}^k \qquad \text{all } i, e. \qquad (2.16)$$

The first term has a positive sign and thereby indicates that the activity uses capacity. The second term has a negative sign and therefore serves to ease the capacity constraint. This shows the double effect of interplant shipments of intermediate products. The activities tighten capacity constraints at the sending plant and ease capacity constraints at the receiving plants.

These interplant shipments of intermediate products provide a means of analyzing the following important economic problem. Countries in common-market or free-trade areas often talk of reaping the benefits from economies of scale by staggering investments over time and space in a complementary fashion. For example, country A may construct an automobile body stamping plant in year one with a capacity substantially above the national automobile production requirements. It will then export to country B for a number of years until its own requirement for automobiles grows to and exceeds the capacity of the plant. At this time country B constructs a new automobile stamping plant and begins exporting to country A. If there are economies of scale so that large plants can produce much less expensively than small plants and if transportation

---

[3] Production processes are said to be subject to economies of scale when the per unit cost of production decreases with increases in the scale of production. Indivisibilities in production processes occur when it is necessary to buy indivisible production units of certain fixed sizes.

[4] The cost coefficients c_{ij}^k for the production and transportation costs of final products include the costs of the intermediate products that go into their manufacture. Therefore, the coefficients a_{il}^k must be viewed as the additional costs to the system of using a unit of intermediate product from another facility rather than manufacturing its own.

costs are relatively low, this sort of arrangement could be of substantial benefit to both countries.

Of course the same situation might apply to several regions within the same country or even to several plants within the same country. Also, it might apply to individual productive units within plants as well as to entire plants.

The incorporation of interplant shipments of intermediate products into the model permits the analysis of this type of investment-staggering plan at the intermediate product as well as at the final product level.

Imports

Imports may serve either of two functions in this model: (1) they may be used to meet final product requirements in the market areas, or (2) they may be used to ease capacity constraints by the importation of certain intermediate products to plants.

Since it may be desirable to import some products but not others and to import these products to some market areas but not to others, we introduce a separate activity into the model for the importation of each product to each market area. We denote these activities by x_j^k (that is, imports of product k to market area j) and observe that they provide an additional means of meeting the market requirement constraints. Thus Equation 2.13, the market requirement constraints, becomes

$$\sum_i w_{ij}^k + x_j^k \geq \sigma_j^k \qquad \text{all } j; k = \kappa + 1, \cdots, K; \qquad (2.17)$$

that is, the market requirements may be met either with domestic production or with imports.

Imports of intermediate products to plants may be used temporarily or for long periods to ease a capacity constraint. For example, a plant with a small blast furnace and steel shop but with a large rolling mill section may import ingot steel until such time as it decides to build more capacity to produce pig iron and ingot steel in its own facilities. Alternatively, the cost of imports of some intermediate products at some plants may be so low relative to the cost of production at the plant that the imports are maintained on a more or less permanent basis.

We denote these imports of intermediate products with the variables v_i^k (that is, imports of intermediate product k to plant i) and note that they serve to ease the capacity constraint in the receiving plant. Thus they enter the capacity constraints with negative coefficients as follows:

$$-\sum_{k=1}^{\kappa} \alpha_i^{ke} v_i^k \qquad \text{all } i, e. \qquad (2.18)$$

As before, the coefficient α_i^{ke} represents the amount of capacity required in productive unit e of plant i to produce a unit of product k.

The cost coefficients for imports of final products represent the real resource cost involved; that is, they include the purchase, transportation, loading, unloading, and insurance cost but exclude the cost of customs duties. This is true if the planning is being done by a national planner who wants to find those means of meeting the product requirements in the market areas that are at the minimum real resource cost.

The coefficients for the imports of intermediate products differ from those for final products in that it is necessary to subtract the cost of producing the imports in the receiving plants from the cost of importing the intermediate products. This is necessary because the cost coefficient c_{ij}^k for the production and transportation cost of the kth product produced at the ith plant and shipped to the jth market area includes the cost of producing the intermediate products. Therefore, the import cost coefficients represent the additional cost to the system of using intermediate products from plants outside of the system rather than using the intermediate products of the plant in question. If some intermediate products can be imported at less cost than they can be produced domestically, these coefficients will of course be negative.

The parameters b_i^k then represent the additional cost to the system of importing intermediate product k to plant i rather than using the intermediate product produced in plant i. Furthermore, we denote with d_j^k the cost of importing a unit of final product k to market area j. The cost of imports may then be written

$$\sum_i \sum_{k=1}^{\kappa} b_i^k v_i^k + \sum_j \sum_{k=\kappa+1}^{K} d_j^k x_j^k. \tag{2.19}$$

Exports

In planning the installation of new capacity, company officials normally have a rather specific market area in mind. They may be forced by indivisibilities and/or economies of scale to buy units that are larger than the existing product requirements in the market area, but they expect that over time the demand in "their" market area will grow enough so that the full capacity of the plant will be required. In the interim, however, they may expect to dump their excess product on foreign markets at prices above their marginal cost but below the prices they charge in their home markets.

The model developed here assumes that the type of behavior just described may be perfectly rational. In the model the industry is forced by the constraints to meet the product requirements for final products either through domestic production or through imports. On the other hand, the industry is not forced by the constraints to export but is permitted to do so if exporting proves to be marginally profitable. This situation is established by calculating the objective function coefficients for exports as follows: the costs of manufacturing the product in question (other than capital costs) and transporting it from the plant to an export port are calculated, and the world market price for the product is subtracted from this cost. If the resulting coefficient is negative, then it is profitable to the system to export the product. However, the decision whether or not to export the product will depend on the capacity available, the cost of imports, the level of domestic requirements, the cost of domestic production, and so on.

Therefore, in the model decisions about exports are made at two levels. In the short run the industry will export if there is sufficient capacity available to do so and if this is the most "profitable" use that can be found for the capacity. In the long run decisions about building additional capacity for exporting purposes will depend on the cost of the investments required to provide the capacity as well as on the margin between world market prices and the domestic cost of production.

The coefficients $\hat{e}_i^k$ are used to represent the expected profit from exporting a unit of product k from plant i. Thus we add the following term to the objective function:

$$\sum_i \sum_{k=1}^{K} \hat{e}_i^k y_i^k. \tag{2.20}$$

This term will be negative for each product and plant for which exporting is a profitable activity.

Since exports use up domestic capacity, we must add the following term to the capacity constraints:

$$\sum_{k=1}^{K} \alpha_i^{ke} y_i^k \qquad \text{all } i, e. \tag{2.21}$$

Exports of both intermediate and final products are included in this term and in the term in Equation 2.20.

In summary, we have a model that now includes (1) multiple intermediate and final products, (2) interplant shipments of intermediate products, (3) imports, and (4) exports. Figure 2.3 gives a diagrammatic representation of the model.

Each arrow now represents activities for shipments of several different products. Arrows to or from outside the system represent exports and imports, respectively, and arrows with solid lines represent shipments of final products while those with dashed lines represent shipments of intermediate products. For example, note that each plant exports both intermediate and final products but imports only intermediate products.

With this model we have a reasonably accurate representation of the

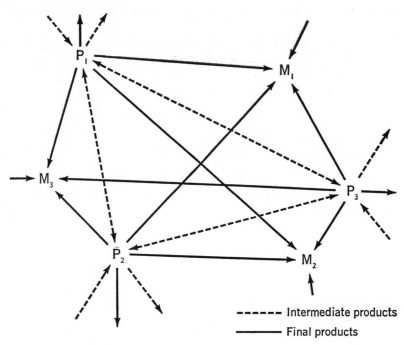

FIGURE 2.3. *A complex spatial model.*

industry at a given point in time. While a single-period model is of little value for making investment decisions, it can be most useful for studying the operations of the system and the effect that changes in transportation or production cost in one part of the system might have on the operation of the rest of the system. In Chapter 4 we present the results of a rather detailed sensitivity analysis on a single-period model. However, before discussing this application of the model we extend the development of the model to include multiple time periods and investment activities.

3

The Multiperiod Model
with Investment Activities

The introduction of the time dimension to the model via multiple time periods and of investment activities with discrete variables is discussed in the opening pages of this chapter. The presentation of the various parts of the model is then completed in a statement of the entire model, followed by a discussion of the assumptions implicit in the model.

Multiple Time Periods

We add the time dimension to our spatial model by including multiple time periods. In diagrammatic terms this may be thought of as repeating Figure 2.3 once for each time period, with the market requirements increasing from time period to time period. Thus, if the time horizon covered by the model is eight years, it might be convenient to divide the time into eight annual periods or four time periods of two years each.

The number of variables and parameters is increased by a multiple of the number of time periods. So the variable w_{ij}^{k} that was used earlier to represent shipments of product k from plant i to market area j becomes a series of variables w_{ij}^{kt}, one for each time period t. In particular, if one can make projections about future transportation cost or production cost, then the cost coefficients for the same activity in two different time periods will be different.

By dividing time in a discrete fashion with multiple time periods an implicit assumption is made that all activities will remain constant *within* a given time period but can change from one time period to the next. For example, in an eight-year model with four time periods each of two years duration there are coefficients $d_j^{k1}, d_j^{k2}, d_j^{k3}$, and d_j^{k4} to represent the

17

cost of each unit of imports of product k to market area j during time periods 1, 2, 3, and 4. Thus it is assumed that one can specify the fixed price that will hold over the two years of each time period or that one can specify the average price that will hold during each time period.

The introduction of multiple time periods into the model brings with it two complications that are of special importance: (1) making cost projections and demand projections, and (2) using time discounting.

In general it may be exceedingly difficult to make good projections for future cost because it requires anticipation of technological changes and shifts in the supply and demand for all the major inputs of goods and services to the industry under investigation. However, in this respect the analyst with a model is no worse off than the analyst without a model.

Demand projections for the final products of the industry can be made using both cross-sectional and time-series data. We denote the requirements by adding a superscript to the market requirement parameter so that σ_j^{kt} represents the requirements in time period t for product k in market area j.

In a multiple-period model our objective is one of minimizing the total present value of cost rather than undiscounted total cost. Therefore, it is necessary to multiply each cost coefficient by the appropriate time discount factor. These factors are denoted D_t and are calculated by

$$D_t = \frac{1}{(1 + \hat{r})^{t^*}},\qquad(3.1)$$

$$t^* = (t - 1)q + (q/2),\qquad(3.2)$$

where t is the time period of the activity, $\hat{r}$ is the social discount rate, and q is the number of years in each time period.

When we discount in this fashion we assume that all cost takes place exactly at the midpoint of each time period. If the costs are evenly distributed over the length of the time period this approach provides a reasonable aproximation though it is not exact.

Investment Activities

If productive units in the process industries could be purchased in any size and were not subject to economies of scale, investment projects to install these units could be represented in our model with continuous nonnegative variables. However, many productive units do not fit the criteria both of being perfectly divisible and of not exhibiting economies of scale. So we focus our attention on methods for incorporating such projects into our analysis.

Investment projects with economies of scale or indivisibilities present special economic and computational problems. Two examples of the special kinds of problems presented by economies of scale are those of spatial and temporal distribution of production facilities. In spatial distribution, strong economies of scale and low transportation costs for final products suggest the establishment of relatively few large and centrally located plants while weak economies of scale and high transportation costs encourage the establishment of many small plants. Likewise, in temporal distribution, strong economies of scale and low capital charges encourage the construction of large plants widely separated over time.

Investment problems that involve economies of scale are interesting not only from an economic but also from a mathematical point of view because the usual methods of optimization cannot be used. Neither classical optimization techniques, nor linear programming, nor quadratic programming techniques can be used to solve this class of problems. The best method yet proposed for their solution is an approximation technique using mixed-integer programming.[1]

Indivisibilities are economically important because many investment projects involve indivisible units like the proverbial bridges and highways. Current engineering practice in the steel industry provides some new examples of important indivisibilities. For example, in some recently constructed steel mills a pair of oxygen converters has been installed to provide the original capacity in the steel shop. Because of the necessity of periodically relining these converters and the desirability of maintaining a steady flow of hot product through the plant, only one converter is kept in operation at a time. When additional capacity is required, a third converter is installed, and then two of the converters are kept in operation at a time while the third is being relined. Thus the addition of the indivisible third converter results in a doubling of the effective capacity of the plant. A second example comes from the rolling mill section of steel mills. In some plants, foundations are built for more stands than are originally installed. The original stands are then operated reversibly with the hot plates rolled back and forth through them. When more capacity is required, the additional stand is installed, and the system of stands is operated in a continuous fashion with the product making only one pass through the mill. Here again the installation of an indivisible productive unit may double the effective capacity.

---

[1] Markowitz and Manne give a discussion of this type of problem and a method of writing the constraints for the approximation method. See H. M. Markowitz and A. S. Manne, "On the Solution of Discrete Programming Problems," *Econometrica,* Vol. 25, No. 1 (January 1957), pp. 19 ff. For a special class of these problems in which there is a fixed requirement at every market, including exports, an algorithm developed by Efroymson and Ray provides an efficient algorithm for solving large problems. See M. A. Efroymson and T. L. Ray, "A Branch and Bound Algorithm for Plant Location," memo., Esso Research and Engineering, 1966.

Indivisibilities present interesting computational problems because most methods of optimization require that the variables be continuous. For example, linear programming requires that all variables be free to take on any nonnegative values. So we direct our attention instead to mixed-integer programming models in which some of the variables, like the projects, are discrete.

As discussed earlier, the methods of analysis presented in this book are directed to investment problems of the sort faced by a planner who is presented with a group of investment projects among which he is to choose those to be executed and to set the time for their execution. Thus we assume that the planner has available information as to (1) the plant and productive unit within the plant where the project would be executed, (2) the cost of executing the project, (3) the increase in the capacity of the productive unit that would result from execution of the project.

For example, a project might be for the addition of the third oxygen converter in a plant that already has two converters installed, or it might be for modifications to an existing blast furnace, or for the installation of a new tinning line. Since from a computational point of view it is desirable to limit the number of investment projects in the model, the planner will enter each project into the model in only those time periods when he thinks it is most likely to be chosen for execution. Furthermore, he should restrict the model so as to permit the execution of each project in only one time period unless the project is of the sort that can be repeated. The planner may make certain adjustments in the projects or return them to the plants for changes that he considers desirable. However, we assume that the changes he can make are slight and that he is more interested in accepting or rejecting projects and scheduling them over time than in modifying the proposals. Thus the role of the central office is one of taking into account the interdependencies between projects while leaving the details of design to the plants or firms.

Therefore, since the planner's task is essentially one of saying yes or no, the investment decision variables are denoted with z_r for the rth project and the z_r's are restricted to the values zero and one.[2] Projects in the solution at the zero level are rejected and those in the solution at the one level are accepted. We use the parameters η_{tr}^{et} to represent the addition to capacity that project r makes in productive unit e of

[2] Scheduling over time is accomplished by putting several activities in the model for each investment project, one activity per time period per project, and constraining the model so as to permit the selection of a particular project in only one time period.

plant i in time period t. Since investments serve to ease the capacity constraints, they enter with a negative sign, and so we add the term

$$-\sum_r \eta_{ir}^{et} z_r \tag{3.3}$$

to the appropriate capacity constraints.[3]

Denoting the cost of project r as f_r and the appropriate discount factor as D_r, the term

$$\sum_r D_r f_r \tag{3.4}$$

is added to the objective function. The discounted cost of the project $D_r f_r$ is calculated as described in the following paragraphs.

Since the outlays for the projects are normally made over a period of several years while the project is being planned, equipment designed and constructed, buildings erected, and equipment installed and tested, the present value of cost calculations should be made by obtaining data on the stream of payments over time and discounting all of the payments to the present. However, as this sort of data is difficult to obtain, it is assumed that the payments are fairly evenly distributed about the midpoint of the gestation period for the project. As an approximation to this distribution, it is assumed that all capital costs are concentrated at the midpoint of the gestation period of the project, and these costs are then discounted to the present.[4]

Since the model has a fixed horizon, one further modification in the treatment of capital cost is necessary to avoid distorting edge effects. If the entire cost of investments made in the later time periods were charged in the planning period, the solutions would tend to favor imports or increased interplant shipments rather than investments. In order to avoid these effects, capital costs are converted to the equivalent uniform payment series and the payments are cut off at the end of the period covered by the model.[5] In effect, the system is forced to pay only for that portion of capital services that is utilized within the fixed time horizon of the model. Or, to express it another way, it is as though the system paid a biannual rent for the use of the capital equipment during the life of the equipment.[6]

[3] If a coefficient η_{ir}^{et} represents the capacity of a project that will go into operation at the beginning of time period τ, then the coefficient will be zero in all constraints for that productive unit in periods $t < \tau$ and greater than zero in all constraints for that productive unit in periods $t \geq \tau$.

[4] Present value as of the midpoint is not the same as the present value of a cost stream that is evenly distributed about the midpoint, but it is a sufficiently accurate approximation for our purposes.

[5] I am indebted to Stephen Marglin for suggesting this approach.

[6] Another approach to the problem of terminal conditions would be to adopt a modification of the approach used by S. Chakravarty and R. S. Eckaus in "Choice

The discounted cost of the investment projects may then be calculated with the following function:[7]

$$D_r f_r = \underset{(a)}{\sum_{t=M}^{H-1} \frac{f_r R}{(1 + R)^t}}$$

$$+ \underset{(b)}{\sum_{t=H}^{\min (H+NZ-1, \, NQ)} f_r \left(\frac{R(1 + R)^{NZ}}{(1 + R)^{NZ} - 1} \frac{1}{(1 + R)^t} \right)}, \quad (3.5)$$

where $D_r f_r$ is the present value of the cost of the project, f_r is the undiscounted cost of the project, R is the discount rate per year, M is the number of the year (the present year being year one) that is at the midpoint of the gestation period of the project. If G is the gestation period of the project in number of years, then $M = H - G/2$. Also H is the number of the year in which the project is put into operation, NZ is the life of the equipment in years, and NQ is the number of the year that is the last period covered by the model. In this equation term (a) represents the discounted cost of using the resources between the midpoint of the gestation period and the beginning of the operation of the project, and term (b) represents the discounted cost of the uniform series of payments. The uniform series of payments is cut off at the end of the period spanned by the model or at the end of the life of the equipment, whichever occurs first.

The Complete Model

In this section we summarize the model with a list of the variables, a list of the parameters, and the equations of the model.

The Variables

Z = the present value in dollars of producing, transporting, and importing the required final bill of goods during the time periods covered by the model.

u_{il}^{kt} = units per year of product k shipped as an intermediate product from plant i to plant l during time period t.

v_i^{kt} = units per year of product k imported during time period t for use as an intermediate product at plant i.

Elements in Intertemporal Planning Models" and "An Approach to Multisectoral Intertemporal Planning Models," both published in P. N. Rosenstein-Rodan, ed., *Capital Formation and Economic Growth* (Cambridge, Mass.: The M.I.T. Press, 1964). The approach used is one of forcing the terminal capacity to be sufficient to maintain the postterminal rates of growth of consumption, government expenditures, and exports.

[7] Henry Jacoby suggested this method of calculating the discounted cost.

w_{ij}^{kt} = units per year of product k produced at plant i and delivered to market area j during time period t.

x_j^{kt} = units per year of product k imported to market area j during time period t.

y_i^{kt} = units per year of product k exported from plant i during time period t.

z_r = investment decision variable.

The Parameters

a_{il}^{kt} = costs (other than capital costs) in dollars per unit for supplying during time period t one unit per year of intermediate product k produced at plant i and delivered to plant l, minus the costs (other than capital costs) of producing one unit per year of intermediate product k over the same length of time in plant l, that is, the extra costs to the system when plant l uses intermediate product k produced at plant i rather than in its own facilities.

b_i^{kt} = cost (other than capital cost) in dollars per unit for importing during time period t one unit per year of product k for use as an intermediate product at plant i, minus the cost (other than capital cost) of producing one unit per year of product k over the same length of time in plant i, that is, the extra cost to the system of importing intermediate product k to plant i rather than producing it in its own facilities.

c_{ij}^{kt} = cost (other than capital cost) in dollars per unit for producing at plant i during period t one unit per year of product k and delivering it to market area j.

d_j^{kt} = cost in dollars per unit for importing to market area j during time period t one unit per year of product k.

e_i^{kt} = value in dollars per unit of export profits gained by the system during time period t from exporting one unit per year of product k from plant i. Export profits per unit are defined as the f.o.b. prices for exports of product k less the sum of the production cost (other than capital cost) and the transportation cost to the port (including loading cost).

f_r = cost of investment r in dollars.

α_i^{ke} = units of capacity required in production unit e of plant i for each unit of product k produced at plant i.

η_{ir}^{et} = units of capacity created in production unit e of plant i in time period t by investment r.

γ_i^e = capacity in the base year of production unit e in plant i, in units of product produced by the unit.

σ_j^{kt} = requirements of market area j for product k during time period t, in units per year.

D_t = discount factor for production-transportation activities in time period t.

D_r = discount factor for investment project r.

The Objective Function

$$\text{Min } Z = \sum_t D_t \left(\underbrace{\sum_i \sum_{l \neq i} \sum_{k=1}^{\kappa} a_{il}^{kt} u_{il}^{kt}}_{(a)} + \underbrace{\sum_i \sum_{k=1}^{\kappa} b_i^{kt} v_i^{kt}}_{(b)} + \underbrace{\sum_i \sum_j \sum_{k=\kappa+1}^{K} c_{ij}^{kt} w_{ij}^{kt}}_{(c)} \right.$$

$$\left. + \underbrace{\sum_j \sum_{k=\kappa+1}^{K} d_j^{kt} x_j^{kt}}_{(d)} - \underbrace{\sum_i \sum_{k=1}^{K} \hat{e}_i^{kt} y_i^{kt}}_{(e)} \right) + \underbrace{\sum_{r=1}^{q} D_r f_r z_r.}_{(f)} \quad (3.6)$$

The objective Function 3.6 states that the object of the problem is to minimize the present value of the cost of producing and transporting the required final bill of goods during the time periods covered by the model. The first summation in the equation sums the cost over the time periods t. Term (a) of the equation represents the "extra" cost to the system of producing intermediate product k in time period t in plant i and shipping it to plant l. The word "extra" refers to the fact that the activity cost a_{il}^{kt} represents the difference between the cost of producing intermediate product k in plant i and shipping it to plant l and the cost of producing it in plant l. Term (b) includes the "extra" cost to the system of importing intermediate product k in time period t rather than producing it in plant i. "Extra" here means the difference between the cost of importing intermediate product k and the cost of producing it at plant i. In both term (a) and term (b) the index runs from 1 to κ, while in terms (c) and (d) it runs from $\kappa + 1$ to K, and in term (e) it runs from 1 to K.

Term (c) of Equation 3.6 represents the cost of producing in all of the $i = 1, 2, \cdots, n$ plants and shipping to all of the $j = 1, 2, \cdots, m$ market areas each of the $k = \kappa + 1, \cdots, K$ final products. Term (d) includes the cost of importing each of the final products $\kappa = \kappa + 1, \cdots, K$ to each of the market areas $j = 1, 2, \cdots, m$. The negative sign preceding term (e) shows that exports are treated as a way to decrease the cost to the system of satisfying the domestic requirements. Finally, the term (f) represents the costs of investments $r = 1, 2, \cdots, q$.

The Constraints

Capacity utilization constraints:

$$\underbrace{\sum_{l \neq i} \sum_{k=1}^{\kappa} \alpha_i^{ke} u_{il}^{kt}}_{(a)} - \underbrace{\sum_{l \neq i} \sum_{k=1}^{\kappa} \alpha_i^{ke} u_{li}^{kt}}_{(a')} - \underbrace{\sum_{k=1}^{\kappa} \alpha_i^{ke} v_i^{kt}}_{(b)} + \underbrace{\sum_j \sum_{k=\kappa+1}^{K} \alpha_i^{ke} w_{ij}^{kt}}_{(c)}$$

$$+ \underbrace{\sum_{k=1}^{K} \alpha_i^{ke} y_i^{kt}}_{(e)} - \underbrace{\sum_{r=1}^{q} \eta_{ir}^{et} z_r}_{(f)} \leq \gamma_i^e \qquad \text{for all } i, e, t. \quad (3.7)$$

The capacity utilization Constraints 3.7 require that in each of the $e = 1, 2, \cdots, s$ productive units in each of the plants in every time period the capacity utilized to produce intermediate goods for other plants, final products for domestic consumption, and intermediate and final products for exports — terms (a), (c), and (e), respectively — must not exceed the capacity available. The negative terms in this set of constraints represent the means of easing these capacity bottlenecks through the receipt of intermediate products from other domestic plants, through imports of intermediate products, and/or through the construction of new capacity — terms (a'), (b), and (f), respectively.

Requirements constraints:

$$\sum_i w_{ij}^{kt} + x_j^{kt} \geq \sigma_j^{kt} \qquad \text{for } k = \kappa + 1, \cdots, K, \text{ and all } j, t. \qquad (3.8)$$

The set of Constraints 3.8 requires that in each time period t, for each final product k and each market area j, the total amount supplied domestically plus the amount imported must be greater than or equal to the requirement.

Nonnegativity constraints:

$$u_{il}^{kt}, v_i^{kt}, w_{ij}^{kt}, x_j^{kt}, y_i^{kt} \geq 0 \qquad \text{all } i, j, k, t, l. \qquad (3.9)$$

Integer constraints:

$$z_r = 0, 1 \qquad r = 1, \cdots, q. \qquad (3.10)$$

The nonnegativity Constraints 3.9 require that all variables in the problem be limited to values greater than or equal to zero. One subset of the variables, the investment variables z_r, is limited by the set of Constraints 3.10 to take on only the values zero or one.

Assumptions Implicit in the Model

Before proceeding to an illustrative application of it, we review the assumptions implicit in the model. First, it is assumed that the price elasticity of demand for the final products is zero; that is, users of the product will purchase the same amount no matter what the price may be. For products for which there are no close substitutes and which have a small range of price changes, this assumption may not be too binding. In situations where it is anticipated that price changes will have large effects on the quantity demanded, quadratic programming models may provide a better method of analysis.

Second, the costs of all activities are assumed to be independent of the level of all other activities. For example, the cost of producing fertilizer in one plant is not affected by the level of production in another plant or in another part of the same plant. Though this assumption does not often appear to be constraining, an example will help to show one case in which it may be constraining and to suggest a method for modifying the assumption. In some investment planning models it may be desirable to choose between alternative technologies for manufacturing the same product. If there are separate activities in the model for investment activities and production activities (as there are in the model developed in this study), and if the different processes would result in substantial changes in the production cost, it will be desirable to establish a link between the investment decision and the production cost. This may be done easily by inserting an additional constraint and an additional slack activity in the model for each linked production process. A negative constant that is greater than the expected activity level of the production activity is placed in the investment activity vector at the row of the additional constraint. A plus one is installed in this row in the production activity vector, and the right-hand side for the constraint is set to zero. The slack activity then contains a single positive unitary entry in the added constraint row. The effect of this additional constraint and slack variable is to force the linked production activity to remain at the zero level unless the investment project is selected for installation; that is, a particular production activity cannot be used unless the capital equipment necessary for that process is installed.[8] Since the modification of this assumption requires only the addition of a single constraint and slack activity, it increases only slightly the computational problem for solving the model.

A third assumption that is implicit in this model is that there is no uncertainty in the system. All product requirements, activity cost, and technical coefficients are assumed to be known and fixed. In an ordinary linear programming model this assumption could be modified through the use of stochastic programming methods. However, there has not as yet been much work done on the combination of stochastic and integer programming methods, so this assumption is a rather difficult one to modify at this point but not of any less importance because of the difficulty.

Fourth, it is assumed that production occurs with fixed proportions and that all inputs are available without limit at a certain fixed price. From the point of view of a single industry or sector of the economy this assumption is likely to be true for a wide range of inputs. For those inputs that are used in large proportions by the industry under investigation it is possible to modify this assumption through the incorporation

[8] For a concise description of the method of setting up these constraints see G. Hadley, *Non-Linear and Dynamic Programming* (Reading, Mass.: Addison-Wesley Publishing Co., Inc., 1964), pp. 252–253.

of piecewise linear segments to approximate either increasing or decreasing unit cost. Markowitz and Manne[9] have demonstrated a method of setting up the constraints for both problems and have shown that the increasing cost case is much simpler in a computational sense than is the decreasing cost case. This is true because the former requires only the addition of more nonnegative variables to the model while the latter requires the use of additional integer variables. As will be discussed later in this study, the addition of each integer variable to a mixed-integer programming problem effectively doubles the size of the computational problem.

Finally, it is assumed that the supply of imports and the demand for exports is perfectly elastic, that is, that foreigners or persons outside of the system are willing to supply all of the imports desired at a certain fixed price and that they are willing to buy at a fixed price all of the exports that the system desires to send out. If the system is a relatively small user of or supplier to the total market of the products concerned, this assumption will not be constraining. If this is not the case, then the assumption can be modified in the manner described in the previous paragraph.

[9] H. M. Markowitz and A. S. Manne, "On the Solution of Discrete Programming Problems," *Econometrica*, Vol. 25, No. 1 (January 1957), pp. 19 ff.

PART II

Application of the Model

4

Description of the
Single-Period Model

This section of the study presents an application of the single-period linear programming model to the production and transportation of flat steel products[1] in Brazil in 1965.[2]

Although there are a number of smaller plants in the area, the industry consists primarily of three steel mills located in the south of Brazil (see Figure 4.1). These plants are (1) COSIPA, Companhia Siderúrgica Paulista, at Piacaguera near Santos, (2) CSN, Companhia Siderúrgica Nacional at Volta Redonda, and (3) USIMINAS, Usinas Siderúrgicas de Minas Gerais S.A., near Ipatinga in the state of Minas Gerais.[3]

CSN at Volta Redonda dates from the Second World War and had an annual ingot capacity of about a million and a half metric tons in 1965. COSIPA and USIMINAS were constructed during 1960–1965; in 1965 COSIPA had an annual ingot capacity of about 800 thousand metric tons and USIMINAS had an annual ingot capacity of about 600 thousand metric tons.

USIMINAS is located near its iron ore source; COSIPA is very near the

[1] The two main groups of steel products are flat products and shapes. Flats include steel plate, hot and cold sheet and strip, and tin plate. Shapes include structural steels, pipes, and bars.

[2] The reader who is not familiar with the terminology of steel technology is referred to Appendix A, which provides a general description of the production of flat steel products.

[3] The data used in this illustrative example were obtained by the author while visiting the three major steel mills in Brazil in January 1965. Appreciation is due the officials of COSIPA, USIMINAS, and CSN for providing data to the author and for permitting him to visit their plants. Likewise, the author is indebted to José Mariano Falcão of the Banco Nacional de Desenvolvimento, Fernando Aguirre Tupper of the Latin American Iron and Steel Institute, and Bruno Leuschner, Armando P. Martijena, and Nuno Fidelino Figueiredo of the Economic Commission for Latin America for providing data and assistance.

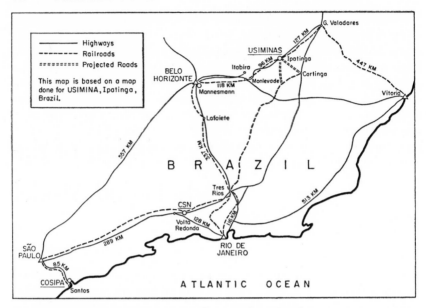

FIGURE 4.1. *Major flat product steel mills in southern Brazil.*

large market of São Paulo and is on the coast; CSN has a compromise location between the ores and the markets. All three facilities use some domestic coal from southern Brazil, which they mix with imported coking coal.

Figure 4.1 shows the road and rail network that links these three plants to one another and to the market areas of São Paulo, Rio de Janeiro, and Belo Horizonte.

In this setting we are interested in the following problem: given (1) the geographic distribution of installed capacity, (2) the geographic distribution of requirements for various flat steel products, (3) the cost of producing both intermediate and final steel products in each of the plants, (4) the cost of shipping the products to other plants or market areas, (5) the cost of imports and the expected profits on exports, and (6) the cost of activities for shipping intermediate products between plants; what is the most efficient pattern of shipments and how might this pattern and its cost change in response to other changes in the system?

Installed Capacity

The capacity of each of the seven major productive units at the three plants in 1965 is given in Table 4.1. These are the parameters that are denoted by $\gamma_i{}^e$ in the model.

At the CSN plant at Volta Redonda almost all capacity was being used to the fullest extent while at the newer plants of COSIPA and USIMINAS, which had not reached the full capacity for which they were designed, there was substantial unused capacity in some units. For example, the capacity of the primary mill at COSIPA was given as about 1.8 million metric tons per year while the capacity of the two oxygen converters in the steel shop was estimated at only .8 million metric tons. The anticipated installation of a third converter that would double the steel shop capacity to 1.6 million metric tons would balance out the capacity in this part of the plant. Table 4.1 shows that a similar situation existed at USIMINAS.

TABLE 4.1 CAPACITY DISTRIBUTION IN 1965
(in millions of metric tons per year)

Productive Unit	COSIPA	USIMINAS	CSN
Blast furnaces*	.72	.90	1.00
Steel shop*	.82	.60	1.42†
Primary mill	1.80	1.80	1.22†
Roughing mill	1.00	1.00	1.25
Hot strip mill	1.50	1.50	1.50
Cold strip mill	.35	.15	.80
Tinning lines	.00	.00	.17‡

* In the single-period model the steel shop and blast furnace were treated as a single productive unit. Since the input of pig iron to steel production is substantially less than one ton of pig iron per ton of ingot steel, the effective constraint on capacity for COSIPA and USIMINAS was the steel shop capacity. The effective constraint for CSN was the blast furnace capacity.

† Reduced by .20 million metric tons per year from actual capacity to account for the fact that roughly this part of the capacity of these units was used for producing materials for manufacturing nonflat products.

‡ In the single-period runs of the model this capacity was increased to .26 million metric tons per year so as to include a tinning line that was expected to be installed in 1966 or 1967.

Though capacity constraints are given in Table 4.1 as a single number, the capacity of a production unit in a steel mill is not an unambiguous concept. First, the capacity of output of a rolling mill depends upon the product mix. A primary mill that is used for producing a high percentage of slabs will have a higher capacity than the equivalent mill required to produce a high percentage of blooms. Second, the capacity of a blast furnace or a steel furnace is affected by changes in the inputs. A blast furnace with a high percentage of sinter or pellet in the charge will produce more than the equivalent furnace charged with lump ore. Likewise, the percentage of scrap charged to an open-hearth furnace affects the output of the furnace. Third, the capacity constraints are not really absolute bottlenecks. For example, if a shortage of blast furnace capacity is the bottleneck in a plant, the percentage of scrap in the steel furnace charge can be increased, or intermediate products of any desired degree of processing may be purchased. While the single-period model permits the shipment of ingot steel between plants, it does not provide for the purchase of other forms of intermediate products such as pig iron, slabs, or coils of hot sheet. Fourth, capacity information given by a company about its production units does not always agree with an economist's notion of what capacity is. Blast furnaces that were installed with a given rated capacity may, in fact, produce as much as twice their rated capacity through increases in their interior dimensions, fuel oil injection, higher blast temperatures and volumes, higher top pressures, more careful sizing of ores, the use of sinter and/or pellets in the charge, or the control of humidity in the furnace. Also, rolling mill capacities may be given as the capacity of the smallest unit in a line. Thus, a hot-strip finishing mill with a capacity of 2 million tons per year that follows a semicontinuous rougher of 1 million tons per year may be classified as having a capacity of only 1 million tons. That is, the capacity stated is given according to the bottleneck. Fifth, capacity figures usually tell nothing at all about the cost of the modifications required to change the capacity of the unit. For example, a semicontinuous rougher installed so that additional stands can be added easily to increase the capacity is really something quite different from a continuous rougher of the same capacity installed in such a small working area that its capacity cannot be increased.

Product Requirements

The market requirements (see Table 4.2), which are denoted by σ_j^k in the model and which are based on an unpublished study of the Latin American Iron and Steel Institute (ILAFA),[4] are at best a rough approximation of reality because a regional breakdown of the requirements for various products was not available at the time of the study.

The ILAFA study gives the apparent consumption of flat products in Brazil in 1962 as 860 thousand tons and shows a growth rate of around 100 thousand tons per year over the period of the previous few years. Assuming that steel consumption is growing at an increasing rate in Brazil, a figure of 1,200 million tons was decided upon for the apparent consumption of flat products in Brazil in 1965. It was assumed that 200

[4] Instituto Latinoamericano del Fierro y el Acero, *Series históricas de consumo aparente, producción, importación y exportación de productos laminados en América Latina, período 1951–1962* (Santiago, Chile, January 1964).

TABLE 4.2   MARKET REQUIREMENTS
(*millions of metric tons per year*)

	São Paulo	Rio de Janeiro	Belo Horizonte
Plates	.02	.16	.02
Hot sheet and strip	.20	.12	.08
Cold sheet and strip	.30	.16	.14
Tinplate	.15	.06	.04

thousand tons of this would be steel plate, 400 thousand tons would be hot sheet and strip, and 600 thousand tons would be cold sheet and strip. Also, it was assumed that the country would consume 250 thousand tons of tin plate in 1965.

Because of the concentration of the shipbuilding industry in Rio de Janeiro, 80 per cent of the country's apparent consumption of steel plate was assigned to that region while the remaining 20 per cent was divided evenly between São Paulo and Belo Horizonte. Forty per cent of the hot sheet and strip requirement was assigned to Rio and 40 per cent to São Paulo, with the remaining 20 per cent going to Belo Horizonte. The centralization of the automobile industry around São Paulo dictated the assignment of 50 per cent of the demand for cold sheet and strip to that market area, with Rio de Janeiro and Belo Horizonte receiving 27 and 23 per cent, respectively. Sixty per cent of the tin plate requirement was assigned to São Paulo, 24 per cent to Rio, and 16 per cent to Belo Horizonte.

The Costs of Production

Form of the Function

Production costs for pig iron and ingot steel were calculated as a linear function of the inputs and the costs of these inputs, using a function of the form

$$u_i{}^k = \sum_h f_i{}^h s_i^{kh} \qquad i = 1, \cdots, n; k = 1, \cdots, p, \qquad (4.1)$$

where $u_i{}^k$ is the cost in U.S. dollars per metric ton for producing a ton of product k in plant i, $f_i{}^h$ is the cost in U.S. dollars per unit for factor input h at plant i, and s_i^{kh} is the specific input in units of the factor input h per metric ton of product k at plant i.

A linear function was used because the two elements of cost, capital cost and labor cost, that would appear to be the most important nonlinear components of cost, were either included elsewhere in the model or accounted for a small share of total cost. Since capacity was fixed, capital costs were treated as sunk costs and therefore excluded. That is, we assumed that the interest charges on the loans secured to purchase the capital equipment already installed must be paid, whether the equipment was used or not. Thus, the capital cost was unaffected by decisions as to when, where, and what to produce.

Labor costs, on the other hand, were assumed to be incurred in a linear relation to the scale of output of each plant. This may be a serious departure from reality. Data on labor costs in the production of steel products are so incomplete that it is impossible at present to judge the validity of this assumption.

The cost of production of a ton of pig iron and a ton of ingot steel is shown in the following sections to be calculated as the sum of some ten to fifteen elements. This type of detailed breakdown of the elements of cost at each plant is possible because technical information on the specific consumption of blast furnaces and steel furnaces is relatively easy to obtain. As it is more difficult to obtain this type of information for each of the many rolling mills in each steel plant, cost breakdowns for the products of each of these mills have not been made. Rather it has been assumed that the greatest part of the variation in the marginal cost of finished steel products, among steel plants in Brazil, can be attributed to differences in the cost of raw materials and to the different technologies used at the various plants, for example, the use of LD (Linz-Donawitz) or open-hearth furnaces.[5] Therefore, calculations of the costs of final products were based only on their ingot steel costs. The cost of each product was calculated as the ingot steel cost at the plant times the input coefficient for the tons of ingot steel required to produce a ton of the final product. Though there is some variability in these coefficients from plant to plant, in this study they have been assumed to be equal for all plants. The coefficients used are 1.28 for steel plate, 1.24 for hot strip and sheet, 1.31 for cold strip and sheet, and 1.40 for tin plate. These coefficients were estimated from data for the plant at Volta Redonda in 1962.

Specific Inputs and Unit Cost of Inputs

A set of specific inputs for the production of pig iron and ingot steel, with the costs of these inputs in the three major plants in Brazil, is shown in Part II of Appendix B. This set, which was used for most of the runs of the model, is based on information obtained from the publications of the Latin American Iron and Steel Institute, some studies

[5] In the mixed-integer programming model that follows in Chapter 5 this admittedly weak assumption was dropped and detailed cost calculations for the conversion cost at each stage of the process were made.

of the Economic Commission for Latin America, annual reports of the steel companies, and data collected by the author while visiting eleven of the major steel mills in Latin America during the latter half of 1964 and the first month of 1965. Part I of Appendix B includes tables of the raw data accompanied by detailed comments on the sources.

Transportation Costs

The transportation-cost function used for calculating rail transport cost is a linear function of distance over a given route.

$$T = a + bX + u \qquad (4.2)$$

where

T = transportation cost over a given route in U.S. dollars per metric ton,

a and b = parameters,

X = distance in kilometers over the route,

u = error term.

The parameters in this function were estimated from data obtained from *Annuário Estatístico do Brasil*. Annual observations in cruzeiros per metric ton for shipments of steel bars and plates on Estrada de Ferro Central do Brasil were used for the five years 1959 to 1963.[6] The data included the freight cost for each year for distances of 100, 200, 300, up to 1,000 kilometers.

It was expected that a function of the form $T = aX^b$, $0 < b < 1$, that is, a function that is linear in the logs of the two variables, would provide an adequate fit to the data. However, in plotting the data it was revealed that Function 4.2 provided a closer fit. Regressions of the form of Function 4.2 were run on the undeflated cruzeiro cost for the five years in order to obtain estimates for the parameters a and b for each year. Then the parameters were deflated, using a price index for manufactured goods other than foods, and finally the parameters were converted from cruzeiros to U.S. dollars by using the free exchange rate for the month in which the observations were made. The results are shown in Table 4.3.

The fits were so good (the minimum R square was greater than .991) one supposes that the rate makers set the rates proportional to the length of haul with a fixed charge for handling and loading costs. If the statistics presented in *Annuário Estatístico do Brasil* reflect the actual rates charged by Estrada de Ferro Central do Brasil, the freight rates failed

[6] The data for 1959–1961 were taken from p. 152 of *Annuário Estatístico do Brasil* for 1961, the data for 1962 from p. 110 of the volume for 1962, and the data for 1963 from p. 208 of the volume for 1963.

to keep up with the inflation. This phenomenon has been observed and commented upon in detail in an article by Baer, Kerstenetzky, and Simonsen.[7] From Table 4.3 it is apparent that the inflation resulted in a decrease in the deflated freight rates and also caused a change in the structure of the rates; that is, the cost of long-distance shipping relative to that of short hauls decreased (note the decline of the parameter b both in deflated cruzeiros and in U.S. dollars).

TABLE 4.3   PARAMETERS FOR THE RAILROAD FREIGHT COST FUNCTION*

Year	Current Cruzeiros (a)	(b)	Deflated Cruzeiros (a)	(b)	U.S. Dollars (a)	(b)	Exchange Rate	Price Index
1959	354.53	1.205	98.5	0.333	2.61	0.00896	136	360
1960	411.20	1.456	81.9	0.307	2.20	0.00778	187	473
1961	493.47	1.747	73.6	0.260	1.87	0.0062	264	671
1962	658.67	2.570	71.3	0.278	1.79	0.00700	367	924
1963†	955.00	3.896	54.9	0.224	1.54	0.00644	620	1740

*The exchange rates used in this table are the free market exchange rates for April 1959, January 1960, May 1961, July 1962, and April 1963 and were taken from *International Financial Statistics*, published by the International Monetary Fund. The price indices are taken from *Annuário Estatístico do Brasil* for 1963, p. 196.

† This last regression excluded the observations for 300 and 400 kilometers.

For most of the experimental runs of the model, the coefficients for 1962 were used so that the function was $T = 1.80 + 0.00700(X)$. Thus, for a shipment of a distance of 500 kilometers the railroad freight cost would have been estimated as $5.30 per ton of steel bars or plates. A set of runs was made using different values of these parameters. This is discussed in Chapter 5.

While Estrada de Ferro Central do Brasil is probably the railroad that carries the largest share of steel products in Brazil, a number of other railroad lines also carry these products. However, as information was not avaliable as to what proportion of the shipments is carried by each of these lines, the freight costs of Estrada de Ferro Central do Brasil have been used for all product shipments on railroads.

Since in some cases the rates charged by a railroad or a trucking concern may not reflect the real social cost of transportation over a given route, the cost calculation computer program written for this study per-

[7] Werner Baer, Isaac Kerstenetzky, and Marios Henrique Simonsen, "Transportation and Inflation: A Study of Irrational Policy Making in Brazil," *Economic Development and Cultural Change*, Vol. XIII, No. 2 (January 1965), p. 188.

mitted the introduction of a fictitious toll cost on certain routes. For example, in the experimental runs made with this model a toll charge of $0.50 per metric ton was added to the freight cost for products transported (by both truck and train) between Santos and the rest of the country, and a charge of $0.40 was added to the cost for all products transported between Rio de Janeiro and the rest of the country. In each of these cases it is necessary to transport the products across the Great Escarpment (a mountainous barrier that separates the south central coast of Brazil from the interior). Similarly, toll charges could have been placed on routes where there is congestion.

As data for truck freight costs were not available, they were estimated from the railroad freight costs in the following manner. For distances of less than 200 kilometers, the truck freight costs were estimated to be 0.9 of the railroad freight costs; for distances of between 200 and 500 kilometers, 1.2 times the railroad freight cost; and for distances of more than 500 kilometers, 1.5 times the railroad freight cost.[8]

Barge and ship freight rates have not been estimated.[9] At present there is little or no shipping of steel products within Brazil by barges or ships; however, in the future there may be such shipments of final products from USIMINAS to Rio de Janeiro and São Paulo. For the moment it has been assumed that all products from the USIMINAS plant will be shipped to these markets by either rail or truck transport.

Table 4.4 gives distances between the markets and plants over feasible routes. The program written to calculate the minimum cost route from each plant to each market employed the cost function already shown in conjunction with the toll charges and the distance table to calculate the cost over each of the possible routes and then to select the least-cost route. Table 4.5 shows the results based on the cost parameters estimated for 1962.

In addition to transportation cost for shipping final products, estimates have been made for the freight cost of shipping ingot steel between plants. These costs are based on the railroad freight cost for final products, and thus probably slightly overestimate the rates actually charged for shipping these intermediate products.

The production-transportation cost coefficients c_{ij}^{k} were then calculated by adding the production cost (see Table B.9 in Appendix B)

[8] The idea of using a step function came from Edgar M. Hoover, *The Location of Economic Activity* (New York: McGraw-Hill Book Company, 1948), pp. 19–20.

[9] I am grateful to Gonzalo Vargas for his assistance in studying ocean freight rates. I regret that the empirical part of the study never advanced to the many-country problem so that this information could be used.

TABLE 4.4 DISTANCES BETWEEN PLANTS AND MARKETS

Plant and Market	Route	Truck (km)	Train (km)	Barge (nautical miles)	Ship (nautical miles)
COSIPA					
São Paulo	1	85	0	0	0
	2	0	85	0	0
Rio de Janeiro	1	5	0	0	220
	2	0	582	0	0
	3	5	0	220	0
Belo Horizonte	1	642	0	0	0
	2	0	837	0	0
USIMINAS					
São Paulo	1	771	0	0	0
	2	0	846	0	0
	3	85	451	480	0
Rio de Janeiro	1	667	0	0	0
	2	0	640	0	0
	3	0	451	260	0
Belo Horizonte	1	214	0	0	0
	2	0	214	0	0
CSN					
São Paulo	1	353	0	0	0
	2	0	353	0	0
Rio de Janeiro	1	146	0	0	0
	2	0	252	0	0
Belo Horizonte	1	473	0	0	0
	2	0	473	0	0

TABLE 4.5 TRANSPORTATION COSTS (*in U.S. dollars per metric ton*)

Plant and Market	Transportation Cost	Route
COSIPA		
São Paulo	2.65	1
Rio de Janeiro	6.37	2
Belo Horizonte	8.15	2
USIMINAS		
São Paulo	7.72	2
Rio de Janeiro	6.28	2
Belo Horizonte	3.29	2
CSN		
São Paulo	4.27	2
Rio de Janeiro	2.93	1
Belo Horizonte	5.11	2

to the transportation cost (see Table 4.5). For example, the coefficient for the activity of producing steel plate at USIMINAS and shipping it to Rio de Janeiro is

$$(\$43.74)(1.28) + \$6.28 = \$55.99 + \$6.28$$
$$= \$62.27 \text{ per metric ton,}$$

where \$43.74 is the cost of production per metric ton of ingot steel at USIMINAS, 1.28 is the specific consumption of ingots in the production of steel plate, and \$6.28 is the transportation cost from USIMINAS to Rio de Janeiro.

TABLE 4.6 ACTIVITY COST FOR PRODUCTION TRANSPORTATION ACTIVITIES c_{ij}^k
(U.S. dollars per metric ton)

Plant and Market	Plate	Hot Sheet and Strip	Cold Sheet and Strip	Tin Plate
COSIPA				
São Paulo	64.82	62.87	66.27	70.64
Rio de Janeiro	68.54	66.59	69.99	74.36
Belo Horizonte	70.32	68.38	71.78	76.15
USIMINAS				
São Paulo	63.71	63.76	65.03	68.96
Rio de Janeiro	62.27	60.52	63.58	67.52
Belo Horizonte	59.29	57.54	60.60	64.54
CSN				
São Paulo	69.56	67.52	71.09	75.68
Rio de Janeiro	68.22	66.18	69.75	74.35
Belo Horizonte	70.40	68.36	71.93	76.52

Imports and Exports

Rather arbitrary assumptions about import costs and expected profits on exports were made for the single-period model. These assumptions were modified for the multiperiod model.

The cost of imports $d_j{}^k$ was set somewhat above domestic cost for the equivalent product, on the assumption that the government would protect the industry. Tariffs collected by the government were assumed to be outside of the system and not used to minimize the total cost of steel in the system. A base price of \$100 per ton for the importation of steel plate to Rio de Janeiro was set. Hot strip was assumed to be more expensive than plate, and cold strip and tin plate were assumed to be progressively more expensive than hot strip. Because the cost desired was the cost of the product delivered to the using firm in the market area, imports for the products to São Paulo were charged \$2 per metric ton more than for the equivalent import to Rio de Janeiro. The similar differential between Belo Horizonte and Rio de Janeiro was assumed to be \$8 per ton.

While there is no constraint in this model on the total amount of imports, such a constraint could be provided either by putting upper bounds on the activity levels of the import activities or by adding another constraint row.

Exports are treated simply as a means of decreasing the total cost in the system. Thus the costs for these activities $\hat{e}_i^k$ are assigned negative values while products requiring greater processing receive greater profits. For the same product the profits received by each firm were assumed to be the same. Table 4.7 gives the cost coefficients for both importing and exporting activities.

TABLE 4.7 IMPORT COST AND EXPECTED EXPORT PROFITS
(U.S. dollars per metric ton)

	Plate	Hot Sheet and Strip	Cold Sheet and Strip	Tinplate
Imports d_j^k				
São Paulo	102	102	112	122
Rio de Janeiro	100	100	110	120
Belo Horizonte	108	108	118	128
Exports e_i^k				
COSIPA	−2	−3	−4	−5
USIMINAS	−2	−3	−4	−5
CSN	−2	−3	−4	−5

Cost of Shipment of Intermediate Products Between Plants

In the single-period model a single intermediate product, ingot steel, was considered. The cost of these activities, a_{il}^k, was calculated by subtracting the cost of producing ingot steel at plant l (the receiving plant) from the cost of manufacturing ingot steel at plant i (the sending plant) and then adding the resulting difference to the cost of transporting the

TABLE 4.8 COSTS OF INTERPLANT SHIPMENTS OF INGOT STEEL
(in U.S. dollars per metric ton)

From	To	Difference in Production Cost	Transportation Cost	Activity Cost a_{il}^k
COSIPA	USIMINAS	4.82	13.72	18.54
COSIPA	CSN	−2.45	9.08	6.63
USIMINAS	COSIPA	−4.82	13.72	8.90
USIMINAS	CSN	−7.27	10.17	2.90
CSN	COSIPA	2.45	9.08	11.53
CSN	USIMINAS	7.27	10.17	17.44

product between the two plants. Table 4.8 gives the transportation cost and the difference between the cost of ingot steel at the two plants.

Capacity Utilization Coefficients

Appendix C provides a description of the single-period model in table format, including a discussion of the capacity utilization coefficients α^{ke}.

An Illustrative Solution

Before proceeding to the test performed on the model, we provide in this section a description of the results from a single illustrative run.[10] The solution shown is not a standard or "best" solution but rather a representative one.

Table 4.9 gives the activity levels for the variables in the solution for this illustrative run. Part 1 of the table gives the activity levels for the variables, and Part 2 gives the activity levels for the slack variables and the simplex multipliers associated with the constraints.

In Part 1 the activity levels of the variables are given in millions of tons shipped. For example, 20 thousand tons of plate were shipped from COSIPA to the São Paulo market area and 160 thousand tons of steel plate were shipped from USIMINAS to the Rio de Janeiro market area. One can see in this particular solution a part of the division of labor that exists between these three steel plants. USIMINAS has a relative specialization in steel plate, COSIPA at Santos in cold sheet and strip, and CSN at Volta Redonda in tin plate.

Only a single import activity appears in this solution, the importation of 2 thousand tons of tin plate to Rio. On the other hand, four export activities appear — the export of hot and cold sheet and strip from both CSN and COSIPA. This corresponds roughly to the situation of the flat products part of the steel industry in Brazil in 1965. Once COSIPA and USIMINAS went into full operation there was something of an excess capacity in hot- and cold-rolled sheet and strip while tin plate capacity continued to be pressed by existing consumption rates.

All variables not among the twenty-one in Table 4.9 are at the zero activity level in this solution.

Activity levels and simplex multipliers are given for the slack variables in Part 2 of Table 4.9. These variables are called "slack" variables because in setting up an original tableau for solving a linear programming

[10] Appreciation is due the M.I.T. Industrial Management Computer Facility for use of their IBM 1620 computer and the IBM 1620-1311 Linear Programming System.

TABLE 4.9 ACTIVITY LEVELS AND SIMPLEX MULTIPLIERS

PART 1: ACTIVITY LEVELS OF ORDINARY VARIABLES

Plant	Market Area	Product	Activity Level (millions of tons)
COSIPA	São Paulo	Plate	.020
USIMINAS	Rio de Janeiro	Plate	.160
USIMINAS	Belo Horizonte	Plate	.020
COSIPA	São Paulo	Hot sheet	.160
USIMINAS	Rio de Janeiro	Hot sheet	.064
USIMINAS	Belo Horizonte	Hot sheet	.080
CSN	Rio de Janeiro	Hot sheet	.096
COSIPA	São Paulo	Cold sheet	.300
USIMINAS	Rio de Janeiro	Cold sheet	.006
USIMINAS	Belo Horizonte	Cold sheet	.140
CSN	Rio de Janeiro	Cold sheet	.154
CSN	São Paulo	Tin plate	.150
CSN	Rio de Janeiro	Tin plate	.058
CSN	Belo Horizonte	Tin plate	.040
Imports	Rio de Janeiro	Tin plate	.002
COSIPA	Exports	Hot sheet	.122
CSN	Exports	Hot sheet	.215
COSIPA	Exports	Cold sheet	.040
CSN	Exports	Cold sheet	.355

PART 2: ACTIVITY LEVELS OF SLACK VARIABLES AND SIMPLEX MULTIPLIERS

Slack Variable		Activity Level (millions of tons)	Simplex Multiplier
Objective function		$96,066,000.00	
Capacity constraints			
COSIPA	Steel shop		2.419
	Primary mill	.980	
	Roughing mill	.280	
	Hot strip mill	.824	
	Cold strip mill		.806
	Tinning line		41.455
USIMINAS	Steel shop		7.460
	Primary mill	1.200	
	Roughing mill	.477	
	Hot strip mill	1.185	
	Cold strip mill		.959
	Tinning line		41.830
CSN	Steel shop	.190	
	Primary mill		2.419
	Roughing mill	.020	
	Hot strip mill	.305	
	Cold strip mill		.806
	Tinning line		37.303
Requirement restraints			
São Paulo	Plate		−70.220
	Hot sheet		−68.170
	Cold sheet		−72.570
	Tin plate		−120.750
Rio de Janeiro	Plate		−73.440
	Hot sheet		−71.390
	Cold sheet		−75.960
	Tin plate		−120.000
Belo Horizonte	Plate		−70.460
	Hot sheet		−68.410
	Cold sheet		−72.980
	Tin plate		−121.590

problem they are added to the matrix in such a way as to take up the slack in the inequalities and convert them to equalities. The reader will note that they are the constraints of the LP matrix described in the previous section.

The first slack variable is the objective function and is given as $96,066,000. This value is the total cost for one year of the production and transportation of flat steel products in Brazil, plus the cost of imports, minus the profits from exports. It will be used repeatedly in later sections of this study to compare the total cost of various alternatives.

The simplex multipliers (or shadow or dual prices) shown in Part 2 of the table provide a measure of the economic value of increasing the capacity of the bottlenecks in the system. Thus *on the margin* each ton of additional capacity in the steel shop at the COSIPA plant will reduce the cost in the system by $2.42 per ton. Glancing down the column of simplex multipliers we find the largest values for the tinning lines. For example, a tinning line constructed at COSIPA (given the assumptions of this model) would decrease the cost in the system *on the margin* by $41.45 for each ton of capacity constructed.

For those production units that do not constitute bottlenecks in the system and have excess capacity there is no benefit to be gained from expansion; therefore the value of the simplex multiplier for these constraints is zero. The unused capacity for these production units is shown in the second column of Part 2 of the table. For example, 980 thousand tons of the installed capacity of 1.8 million tons of capacity of the primary mill at COSIPA would not be used.

The simplex multiplier has a slightly different interpretation for the market requirement constraints. It provides a measure of the cost to the system of an expansion in the requirement for a product in a market area. An expansion in the requirement for plate in the São Paulo market area would cost the system $70.22 per ton. An expansion in the requirement for tin plate in São Paulo (due to the fact that importation of tin plate is necessary in this solution) would cost the system $121.75 per ton.

So cost in the system can be decreased either through additional investment to increase the capacity of the bottleneck production units or through the restriction of demand. The magnitude of the simplex multipliers gives an index of the effect that could be expected from each of the alternative measures.

The use of shadow prices in investment decisions must be made with care. An example will suffice to show this. The current shadow price for tin plate in each of the three markets is about $120 per ton and the value of the simplex multiplier for each of the tinning lines is in the neighborhood of $40; however, if the capacity at any one of these mills was expanded by more than 2 thousand tons (the amount of tin that is being imported) or if the market requirement for tin plate in the system was reduced by more than 2 thousand tons, the shadow prices would fall to about $80 per ton (near the domestic cost of production), and the simplex multipliers for the tinning lines would decrease substantially. Therefore, in using shadow prices one must be careful to investigate the range over which the shadow price is likely to hold.

Table 4.10 provides an indication of the stability of the solution of

TABLE 4.10   STABILITY OF THE SOLUTION
 (*U.S. dollars per metric ton*)

Activity	Current Cost	Highest Cost	High Variable
COSIPA, São Paulo, Plate	67.12	71.18	CSN, São Paulo, Plate
USIMINAS, Rio de Janeiro, Plate	63.89	63.98	CSN, Rio de Janeiro, Plate
USIMINAS, Belo Horizonte, Plate	60.91	65.57	CSN, Belo Horizonte, Plate
COSIPA, São Paulo, Hot	65.17	69.14	CSN, São Paulo, Hot
USIMINAS, Rio de Janeiro, Hot	62.14	66.66	USIMINAS, São Paulo, Plate
USIMINAS, Belo Horizonte, Hot	59.16	63.73	CSN, Belo Horizonte, Hot
CSN, Rio de Janeiro, Hot	68.39	68.48	CSN, Rio de Janeiro, Plate
COSIPA, São Paulo, Cold	68.57	72.71	CSN, São Paulo, Cold
USIMINAS, Rio de Janeiro, Cold	65.20	66.19	USIMINAS, Cold sheet mill slack
USIMINAS, Belo Horizonte, Cold	62.22	66.79	CSN, Belo Horizonte, Cold
CSN, Rio de Janeiro, Cold	71.96	72.11	COSIPA, Rio de Janeiro, Cold
CSN, São Paulo, Tin	77.30	78.55	Imports, São Paulo, Tin
CSN, Rio de Janeiro, Tin	76.55	80.84	COSIPA, Rio de Janeiro, Tin
CSN, Belo Horizonte, Tin	78.14	82.63	COSIPA, Belo Horizonte, Tin
Imports, Rio de Janeiro, Tin	120.00	121.25	Imports, São Paulo, Tin
COSIPA, Exports, Hot	−3.00	−2.69	COSIPA, Rio de Janeiro, Plate
CSN, Exports, Hot	−3.00	−1.94	CSN, Exports, Plate
COSIPA, Exports, Cold	−4.00	−3.85	COSIPA, Rio de Janeiro, Cold
CSN, Exports, Cold	−4.00	−3.17	CSN, Cold sheet mill slack

the model to changes in the parameters. The column "Current Cost" is the activity cost for the vector and the column "Highest Cost" is the cost to which that activity could rise before it would be replaced in the solution by another activity. In the current solution the market for plate in the São Paulo area is being served by the COSIPA plant near Santos at a cost to the plant (and to the system) of $67.12 per ton. However, the plant could charge $71.18 per ton for its plate delivered in São Paulo before its competitor at Volta Redonda (see column "High Variable") could undersell it. From this table one could calculate the rents that might accrue to each plant. This type of information can be invaluable both to private competitors and to tax authorities who are eager to scoop up all rents in the system.

TABLE 4.11 REDUCED COST
(U.S. dollars per metric ton)

Variable	Current Cost	Reduced Cost	Difference
COSIPA, USIMINAS, Steel	18.54	13.50	5.04
COSIPA, CSN, Steel	6.63	9.05	−2.42
USIMINAS, COSIPA, Steel	8.90	13.94	−5.04
USIMINAS, CSN, Steel	2.90	10.36	−7.46
CSN, COSIPA, Steel	11.52	9.10	2.42
CSN, USIMINAS, Steel	17.43	9.97	7.46
COSIPA, Rio de Janeiro, Plate	70.66	.32	70.34
COSIPA, Belo Horizonte, Plate	72.44	5.08	67.36
USIMINAS, São Paulo, Plate	65.33	4.66	60.67
CSN, São Paulo, Plate	71.18	4.06	67.12
CSN, Rio de Janeiro, Plate	70.43	.09	70.34
CSN, Belo Horizonte, Plate	72.02	4.66	67.36
COSIPA, Rio de Janeiro, Hot	68.71	.32	68.39
COSIPA, Belo Horizonte, Hot	70.50	5.09	65.41
USIMINAS, São Paulo, Hot	63.58	4.66	58.92
CSN, São Paulo, Hot	69.14	3.97	65.17
CSN, Belo Horizonte, Hot	69.98	4.57	65.41
COSIPA, Rio de Janeiro, Cold	72.11	.15	71.96
COSIPA, Belo Horizonte, Cold	73.90	4.92	68.98
USIMINAS, São Paulo, Cold	66.65	4.84	61.81
CSN, São Paulo, Cold	72.71	4.14	68.57
CSN, Belo Horizonte, Cold	73.55	4.57	68.98
COSIPA, Rio de Janeiro, Tin	76.48	4.29	72.19
COSIPA, Belo Horizonte, Tin	78.27	4.49	73.78
USIMINAS, São Paulo, Tin	70.58	5.26	65.32
USIMINAS, Rio de Janeiro, Tin	69.14	4.57	64.57
Imports, São Paulo, Plate	102.00	31.78	70.22
Imports, São Paulo, Hot	102.00	33.83	68.17
Imports, São Paulo, Cold	112.00	39.43	72.57
Imports, São Paulo, Tin	122.00	1.25	120.75
Imports, Rio de Janeiro, Plate	100.00	26.56	73.44
Imports, Rio de Janeiro, Hot	100.00	28.61	71.39
Imports, Rio de Janeiro, Cold	110.00	34.04	75.96
Imports, Belo Horizonte, Plate	108.00	37.54	70.46
Imports, Belo Horizonte, Hot	108.00	39.59	68.41
Imports, Belo Horizonte, Cold	118.00	45.02	72.98
Imports, Belo Horizonte, Tin	128.00	6.41	121.59
COSIPA, Exports, Plate	−2.00	1.10	−3.10
USIMINAS, Exports, Plate	−2.00	7.55	−9.55
CSN, Exports, Plate	−2.00	1.10	−3.10
USIMINAS, Exports, Hot	−3.00	6.25	−9.25
USIMINAS, Exports, Cold	−4.00	6.76	−10.76
COSIPA, Exports, Tin	−5.00	42.81	−47.81
USIMINAS, Exports, Tin	−5.00	50.43	−55.43
CSN, Exports, Tin	−5.00	38.45	−43.45

One begins to get some idea of the complexities of the readjustments in the system in response to a change in a single parameter by looking at the fifth row in this table. If the cost of supplying hot strip and sheet from USIMINAS to Rio de Janeiro rose above $66.65, then cost could be minimized in the system by having USIMINAS use its capacity for supplying plate to São Paulo. Some other plant, perhaps the one that lost the plate market in São Paulo, will pick up the extra requirement for hot strip and sheet in Rio de Janeiro.

A quick glance down the two columns of current cost and highest cost reveals that the geographical spread of the three major steel plants for flat products in Brazil gives the market situation (of the model) a certain degree of stability. For nine of the fourteen domestic market variables the separation between the current cost and the highest cost is greater than $2 per ton. At the same time this form of stability indicates that the plants are in a position to reap substantial rents if provided a free-enterprise situation in which to do so.

The last section of the output, the reduced cost (Table 4.11), is similar to the previous section in that it shows how much the cost of an activity which is not in the solution must be reduced before that activity can enter the solution. From the previous discussion we know that CSN could take the plate market in São Paulo away from COSIPA if it could reduce its cost for producing plate to $67.12. Table 4.11 confirms that fact (see row "CSN, São Paulo, Plate" and column "Difference") by showing that CSN would have to reduce its cost by $4.06 per ton to secure the market. Likewise, the table reveals how low the cost of imports must go to compete in the domestic market and how high the profits from exporting must go to make it profitable to export a product that is not currently exported. While it would benefit the system to export steel plate from Santos if the profits to be gained from such enterprise were only $1.09 greater, there would be no benefit from exporting tin plate unless the international price increased by $40 to $50 per ton.

One other comment about the first six rows of this table. The column "Reduced Cost" indicates the magnitude by which the cost of shipping ingot steel would have to be reduced before it would be worth while to engage in the shipment of intermediate product. In one of the test runs we decreased steel capacity at the COSIPA plant and hot and cold strip mill capacity at the USIMINAS plant to zero (the situation that existed in January of 1965), and just as might be expected we began to get some shipment of intermediate product in the system. We shall return to this in the next chapter in a discussion of the tests that were conducted with the model.

5

Tests with the
Single-Period Model

This chapter shows some of the properties of the linear programming model and its usefulness as an analytical tool for studying a variety of policy problems. The six tests discussed here involve changes in one or a group of the parameters of the model while holding others constant to determine the effects of the changes. The tests were chosen both for their usefulness in investigating the properties of the model and for their similarity to economic policy problems of the Brazilian flat-product steel industry. The reader who is more interested in the structure of multi-period models than the testing of single-period models should skip to the beginning of Chapter 6.

The first test "requirement shift" was a study of the effects on the system of locating a new automobile plant in Brazil. The model was run repeatedly with the new plant located first in one market area and then shifted to each of the other market areas in turn. Analyses were made of the changes in activity levels, shadow prices, total system cost, and profits accruing to the plants as this "chunk of product requirements" was moved around in the system.

Increases in the requirement levels in all markets simultaneously with constant production capacity was the subject of the second study. Market requirements were increased in five steps from their original levels to three and a half times their original levels.

In the third test changes in factor cost and in technology were examined. For example, a test was made of the effects on the system of the introduction of fuel oil injection in the blast furnace at the COSIPA plant.

The ability of the model to respond with shipments of intermediate

49

products when part of the production capacity in the system was shut down was studied in the fourth test.

If all three plants in the system were simultaneously to request import permits to purchase a new tinning line and the government were to decide that only one new tinning line was needed in the country at the time, which request should be granted? This is the subject of the fifth test.

Finally, a series of runs was made with the model to study the effects of changes in the transportation cost for final products. Unless specific mention is made of a change in a parameter or group of parameters, their values will be the same as those shown in Tables 5.3 through 5.6.

Requirement Shift

Nearness to automobile plants, with their large requirements for hot- and cold-rolled sheet and strip as well as other steel products, is considered one of the prime determinants of the profitability of a steel plant location. To obtain more insight into the importance of this effect, we decided upon an automobile plant size "chunk of product requirement" and moved it around in the system, then we doubled the size of the chunk and moved it around in the system again, solving the linear programming problem at each step.

We made the assumption that a small automobile uses about a half ton of flat steel products (three-fourths of this being cold-rolled products and one-fourth hot-rolled products) and that a reasonable size automobile plant would produce 200 thousand units (production of automobiles and trucks in Brazil in 1964 was about 1 million units), and then determined an automobile plant size "chunk of product requirement" to include 25 thousand tons of hot-rolled products and 75 thousand tons of cold-rolled products.

These quantities were added to the existing requirements for these products first in the São Paulo market area, then the Rio de Janeiro area, and finally the Belo Horizonte area. The amount was then doubled to 50 thousand tons of hot-rolled and 150 thousand tons of cold-rolled products and the tests were repeated.

Table 5.1 gives the value of the objective function for each step as well as the average cost per ton of product.

The total cost of operating the steel system is seen to be relatively unaffected by the location of the automobile plant at the three different market areas. São Paulo is the best location by a margin of $170 thousand a year — that is, about $1 per automobile. This small effect is not a particularly surprising result since there is a steel mill located near

TABLE 5.1   REQUIREMENT SHIFT TEST: EFFECT ON TOTAL SYSTEM COST AND
AVERAGE COST PER TON OF PRODUCT

| | Original Solution | New Automobile Plant | | | | | |
| | | 100 Thousand Tons | | | 200 Thousand Tons | | |
		São Paulo	Rio de Janeiro	Belo Horizonte	São Paulo	Rio de Janeiro	Belo Horizonte
Total cost (in millions of U.S. dollars)	93.446	100.538	100.708	100.767	107.817	107.970	108.117
Average cost (in U.S. dollars per metric ton)	64.44	64.86	64.96	65.01	65.34	65.44	65.53

each of the market areas and there is not a great variation between these plants in the cost of producing steel.

If on the other hand the automobile plant had been located in one of the southernmost states of Brazil or in the northwest part of the country, the difference in the total system cost would have been more striking. Also, even within the area considered, the difference might have been more striking if all hot sheet and strip and all cold sheet and strip had not been treated as homogeneous commodities. In fact, the width and quality of finish of hot- and cold-rolled products is a matter of paramount importance to the automobile industry. A more detailed product breakdown than provided by the four products used in this study would be necessary to catch these distinctions.

The increase in the average cost per ton of product (see Table 5.1) resulted from the loss of some export profits (due to the increase in the total product requirement in the country).

Table 5.2 shows the "profits" accruing to the steel plants under dif-

TABLE 5.2   REQUIREMENT SHIFT TEST: "PROFITS" ACCRUING TO PLANTS (*in millions of U.S. dollars*)

		New Automobile Plant		
Plant	Original Solution	São Paulo	Rio de Janeiro	Belo Horizonte
COSIPA	2.26	3.84	2.26	2.32
USIMINAS	4.33	4.33	4.33	5.08
CSN	3.24	3.24	3.24	3.24

ferent locations of the new automobile plant. The "profits" were calculated as follows. The cost of each activity in the solution was subtracted from the shadow price for the appropriate good and market to give a unit "profit." [1] To calculate the total profits accruing to each plant, the unit profits were multiplied by the activity levels of the solution and then the profits for each plant were summed. Though a part of the profits should be attributed to transportation and a part to production, they have been treated here as though the steel plants owned the means of transportation.

The first column of Table 5.2 shows the profits by plant for the original solution before the new automobile plant is added to the system.

[1] These "profits" are not the same as those normally discussed but are rather more like economic rents. Normal profits are calculated by subtracting total cost (including capital cost) from total revenues. In the definition of "profits" used here the cost (other than capital cost) of producing and transporting a good are subtracted from the shadow price in the market area.

The remaining three columns give the profits for the case in which a 200-thousand unit automobile plant (100 thousand tons of steel products) is located first at São Paulo, then at Rio de Janeiro, and finally at Belo Horizonte.

With the original conditions, the COSIPA plant at Santos would gain a profit of $2.26 million, the largest part of its profit coming from the sale of cold sheet and strip. USIMINAS, on the other hand, would have a profit almost twice that of COSIPA, and CSN a profit about one and a half times that of COSIPA. The high profits for USIMINAS occurred because of the low assembly cost of raw materials there and its proximity to the Belo Horizonte market, which was protected by distance from the products of other plants. On the coast COSIPA and CSN both had excess capacity and were forced to export, thereby bringing their unit profits down to the level of the profits gained from exporting. (In the model the plants were not permitted to make greater profits on domestic sales than on exports.) Another reason for the high profits of USIMINAS was that under the assumptions of the model on input cost, the specific consumption of raw materials, the transportation cost, and so on, USIMINAS could deliver steel products to Rio de Janeiro at a lower cost than CSN could. For example, USIMINAS could deliver hot sheet and strip to Rio de Janeiro for about $6 per ton less than CSN could. Thus USIMINAS could garner the high profit domestic markets and force CSN into the lower profit export markets.

Column 2 of Table 5.2 shows that location of the new automobile plant near São Paulo added substantially to the profits of COSIPA, increasing them from $2.26 to $3.84 million. This resulted in large part from the increase in the shadow price of cold sheet and strip at São Paulo. This jump in the shadow price occurred because the new automobile plant at São Paulo caused the requirement for cold sheet and strip in that market to exceed the capacity of the cold strip mill in the nearby Santos plant of COSIPA.

Location of the automobile plant at Rio de Janeiro rather than at São Paulo resulted in no changes of profit from the original solution. Though at first this seems to violate one's intuition about the matter, it follows from the fact that the original solution remains feasible with the change in the demand conditions. Readjustments could be made in the levels of activities already in the solution, and it was not necessary to introduce any of the more expensive activities that had been excluded from the original optimal solution.

The building of the new automobile plant at Belo Horizonte resulted in a substantial increase in profits for USIMINAS and a slight change in profits for the other two plants. Of the three possible locations, São Paulo offered the minimum total cost and the maximum profit to the system. However, the location giving the second greatest profit to the system (Belo Horizonte) is the third-ranking solution by the cost-minimizing standard.

We now turn our attention from a study of the effects of "requirement shift" to an analysis of the effects of increases in *total* product requirement.

Requirement Increase

By holding capacity constant while increasing the product requirement in the entire system we provide insight into where in the system bottlenecks may arise in the future. Since capital costs are not included, the model cannot be used for making *exact* decisions on the time and place to add to capacity; however, it can reveal future bottlenecks as indicators for investment.

Part 1 of Table 5.3 gives the requirements vector used in the base run

TABLE 5.3   PARAMETERS FOR REQUIREMENTS INCREASE TEST

PART 1: REQUIREMENT LEVELS
(*million metric tons*)

Market	Plate	Hot	Cold	Tin
São Paulo	.020	.200	.300	.150
Rio de Janeiro	.160	.120	.160	.060
Belo Horizonte	.020	.080	.140	.040

PART 2: TRANSPORTATION COST
(*U.S. dollars per metric ton*)

Plant	Market	Cost
COSIPA	São Paulo	4.95
COSIPA	Rio de Janeiro	8.49
COSIPA	Belo Horizonte	10.27
USIMINAS	São Paulo	9.34
USIMINAS	Rio de Janeiro	7.90
USIMINAS	Belo Horizonte	4.91
CSN	São Paulo	5.89
CSN	Rio de Janeiro	5.13
CSN	Belo Horizonte	6.73

of the experiment. This vector was increased by factors of 1½, 2, 2½, and 3 in the runs of the model. The total product requirement for the first run was 1.450 million tons and was increased in steps to 2.175, 2.900, 3.625, and 4.350 million tons.

All parameters of the model were the same for this test as for the previous test, with the following exceptions. The capacity of the tinning line at CSN was assumed to be 260 thousand tons per year instead of 280 thousand tons per year. This assumption resulted in the tin imports already discussed. Also, a somewhat higher transportation cost was used [2] (see Part 2 of Table 5.3) and the capacity of the blast furnace–steel shop and of the primary mill at CSN was assumed to be 200 thousand tons greater than in the previous runs.[3] Thus in the first test that part of the capacity in the blast furnace, steel shop, and primary mill at CSN that is used for producing materials for rolling into shapes instead of flats was subtracted out of the total capacity available. All of these changes were held constant over the five runs made in this test.

Looking first at the effect on total cost in the system, one observes (see the first two rows of Table 5.4) that total cost increased and that average cost per ton of product also increased but at a decreasing rate. This resulted from the decrease in exports (until they ceased altogether) and the steadily increasing share of imports in total national consumption.

The lower part of Table 5.4 shows that as the market requirements increased, first tin plate, then cold sheet and strip and steel plate, and finally hot sheet and strip were imported. This pattern resulted from the relative shortage of tin plate capacity and surplus of hot strip mill capacity. Moving to the top of the table one can see the effect on the activity vector for the shipment of ingot steel from CSN to the COSIPA plant at Santos. At the original level of demand and at one and a half times that level it was not efficient to make the shipment of the intermediate product. However, as the average cost of products in the system rose, it became economic to ship the intermediate product and thereby to make more efficient use of the excess rolling capacity at the COSIPA plant. The amount shipped in this case was determined by the fact that the blast furnace and steel shop capacity at CSN was 190 thousand tons greater than the capacity of the primary mill.

The activity levels of the variables showed a tendency, as the requirements increased for each plant, to concentrate on serving the nearest market area, so that interior markets would be served by domestic production and imports would go to markets near ports.

---

[2] This higher transportation cost resulted from an error in the calculations of this element of cost. However, the higher transportation cost was held constant across all runs in this and the other test in which it was used.

[3] In these runs no allowance was made for the fact that about 200 thousand tons of the capacity of the blast furnace–steel shop and of the primary mill are used for manufacturing materials for use in products other than flat products.

TABLE 5.4 REQUIREMENTS INCREASE TEST: ACTIVITY LEVELS OF VARIABLES
(*millions of tons*)

Vector	Requirement Level				
	1	1½	2	2½	3
Objection function (in millions of U.S. dollars)	96.220	155.776	226.889	304.749	383.352
Average cost per ton (in U.S. dollars per ton)	66.36	71.50	78.30	83.10	88.10
CSN, COSIPA, Ingots	—	—	.190	.190	.190
COSIPA, São Paulo, Plate	.020	.002	.040	—	—
COSIPA, Rio de Janeiro, Plate	.054	—	.014	—	—
USIMINAS, Rio de Janeiro, Plate	.106	.173	.125	—	—
USIMINAS, Belo Horizonte, Plate	.020	.030	.040	.050	.060
CSN, São Paulo, Plate	—	.028	—	.043	—
CSN, Rio de Janeiro, Plate	—	.067	.069	—	—
COSIPA, São Paulo, Hot	.200	.300	.400	.456	.456
USIMINAS, Rio de Janeiro, Hot	.120	—	—	.078	.028
USIMINAS, Belo Horizonte, Hot	.080	.120	.160	.200	.240
CSN, São Paulo, Hot	—	—	—	.044	.144
CSN, Rio de Janeiro, Hot	—	.180	.240	.222	.166
COSIPA, São Paulo, Cold	.300	.340	.340	.340	.340
COSIPA, Rio de Janeiro, Cold	.040	—	—	—	—
USIMINAS, Rio de Janeiro, Cold	.006	—	—	—	—
USIMINAS, Belo Horizonte, Cold	.140	.146	.146	.146	.146
CSN, São Paulo, Cold	—	.110	.260	.305	.235
CSN, Rio de Janeiro, Cold	.115	.240	.115	—	—
CSN, Belo Horizonte, Cold	—	.064	.134	.204	.274
CSN, São Paulo, Tin	.150	.188	.168	.148	.128
CSN, Rio de Janeiro, Tin	.058	—	—	—	—
CSN, Belo Horizonte, Tin	.040	.060	.080	.100	.120
Imports, São Paulo, Plate	—	—	—	.007	.060
Imports, Rio de Janeiro, Plate	—	—	.113	.400	.480
Imports, Rio de Janeiro, Hot	—	—	—	—	.166
Imports, São Paulo, Cold	—	—	—	.105	.325
Imports, Rio de Janeiro, Cold	—	—	.205	.400	.480
Imports, São Paulo, Tin	—	.037	.132	.227	.322
Imports, Rio de Janeiro, Tin	.002	.090	.120	.150	.180
COSIPA, Exports, Hot	.026	—	—	—	—
CSN, Exports, Hot	.311	.033	—	—	—
CSN, Exports, Cold	.395	.095	—	—	—

The change in flows in various parts of the system was not a simple expansion that kept pace with the increase in total requirements in the system. What appeared was a transportation planner's nightmare. Some flows increased, then leveled off and decreased, others started and stopped and started again, others remained static, and still others rose steadily. Had a price response of the transportation sector been built into the model, the changes in the levels of the activities would have been less sharp. Also, rigidities in the system such as taste preferences for the products of one plant over those of another plant would have reduced the sharpness of the changes shown by Table 5.4. Finally, the magnitudes of the changes in product requirement used here were large. Changes of the magnitude shown in the table would be expected to require fifteen to twenty years.

For planning over shorter periods of time an experiment of this type could be most helpful to transportation planners. Also, the experiment could be modified easily to account for increases in capacity over time, with a linear programming run being made for each time period.

Table 5.4 also demonstrates how useful this kind of experiment could be for the economist concerned with the balance of payments. In countries where steel products represent a substantial portion of imports or exports, disaggregated projections on a product by product basis could be made with this type of model. For such planning it would be important to make a modification to the model by adding a constraint row for each imported raw material used in the production of steel products. Then the solution would provide an estimation of the total amount of each of the raw material imports required.

Table 5.5 shows the increase in shadow prices on products as the national requirement increases. Discontinuities in changes in the shadow

TABLE 5.5   REQUIREMENTS INCREASE TEST: SHADOW PRICES
(U.S. dollars per ton)

Market and Product	Requirement Level					Import Prices
	1	$1\frac{1}{2}$	2	$2\frac{1}{2}$	3	
São Paulo						
Plate	70.22	74.95	96.46	102.00	102.00	102
Hot	68.17	72.95	93.59	99.00	100.75	102
Cold	73.10	77.40	110.76	112.00	112.00	112
Tin	120.75	122.00	122.00	122.00	122.00	122
Rio de Janeiro						
Plate	73.76	74.20	100.00	100.00	100.00	100
Hot	71.70	72.04	97.04	98.25	100.00	100
Cold	76.64	76.64	110.00	110.00	110.00	110
Tin	120.00	120.00	120.00	120.00	120.00	120
Belo Horizonte						
Plate	70.78	71.28	97.02	98.18	99.99	108
Hot	68.72	69.15	94.14	95.27	97.02	108
Cold	73.66	78.24	111.60	112.84	112.84	118
Tin	121.59	122.84	122.84	122.84	122.84	128

prices occurred between those steps where importation of a given product became necessary. For example, there was a sharp jump in the shadow prices for steel plate, hot sheet and strip, and cold sheet and strip between steps 1½ and 2, which corresponded to the initiation of imports of steel plate and cold sheet and strip in step 2.

Changes in Cost Parameters[4]

In this test an analysis was made of the effects on the system of some possible technical changes in the production methods. For example, it was shown that under the assumptions of the model there would be a sharp difference in the benefits to the country and to each plant from the installation of oil injection in the blast furnace at COSIPA. The country at large would reap a large benefit from the change and would do well to subsidize the investment at COSIPA, but the competing firm of USIMINAS would suffer a substantial loss in profits and COSIPA would be able to force down the prices on several products.

An analysis was also made of the effects on the system of the installation of a sinter plant at USIMINAS. It was shown that under the assumptions of the model the profit gain to USIMINAS from such an action would be about the same as the benefit to the country at large, so that subsidization by the central government would not be advised in this case.

Shipments of Intermediate Product

As of the beginning of 1965, COSIPA had its rolling mills in operation but had not completed the construction of the LD converters and the blast furnace. USIMINAS, on the other hand, had completed the installation of its steel shop and its blast furnaces but did not have all of its rolling mills in operation. This situation gave rise to a shortage of ingot steel at COSIPA and a surplus at USIMINAS. The result was that COSIPA was buying ingot steel from USIMINAS as well as from CSN.

Most experimental runs made with this model assumed that the ingot steel production capacity at COSIPA and the full rolling capacity at USIMINAS were in operation; however, in one run the steel shop–blast furnace at COSIPA and the hot and cold strip mills at USIMINAS were assigned zero capacity. Also, the blast furnace capacity at USIMINAS was reduced to 485 thousand tons per year to reflect the reality that only one of the USIMINAS blast furnaces was in operation. All other parameters of the model were the same as those for the first experiment de-

---

[4] Results of these tests are reported in detail in David A. Kendrick, "Programming Investment in the Steel Industry," Ph.D. dissertation, Department of Economics, Massachusetts Institute of Technology, Cambridge, Mass., 1966.

scribed, that is, lower transportation cost, higher tinning line capacity at CSN, and lower blast furnace–steel shop and primary mill capacity at CSN (this last item accounting for the fact that a part of the capacity of these two units at CSN was used to produce shapes rather than flats).

As was expected the solution included a shipment of ingot steel from USIMINAS to COSIPA (229 thousand tons) and a shipment of ingot steel from CSN to COSIPA (203 thousand tons). Table 5.6 shows the activity

TABLE 5.6 INTERMEDIATE PRODUCT SHIPMENT TEST: ACTIVITY LEVELS OF VARIABLES (*millions of metric tons*)

Activity	Original Run	Modified Run
USIMINAS, COSIPA, Steel	—	.229
CSN, COSIPA, Steel	—	.203
COSIPA, São Paulo, Plate	.020	—
USIMINAS, São Paulo, Plate	—	.020
USIMINAS, Rio de Janeiro, Plate	.160	.160
USIMINAS, Belo Horizonte, Plate	.020	.020
COSIPA, São Paulo, Hot	.200	.200
USIMINAS, Rio de Janeiro, Hot	.064	—
USIMINAS, Belo Horizonte, Hot	.080	—
CSN, Rio de Janeiro, Hot	.056	.120
CSN, Belo Horizonte, Hot	—	.080
COSIPA, São Paulo, Cold	.300	.140
USIMINAS, Rio de Janeiro, Cold	.005	—
USIMINAS, Belo Horizonte, Cold	.140	—
CSN, São Paulo, Cold	—	.160
CSN, Rio de Janeiro, Cold	.155	.160
CSN, Belo Horizonte, Cold	—	.140
COSIPA, São Paulo, Tin	.001	—
USIMINAS, Belo Horizonte, Tin	.001	—
CSN, São Paulo, Tin	.149	.150
CSN, Rio de Janeiro, Tin	.060	.060
CSN, Belo Horizonte, Tin	.039	.040
COSIPA, Exports, Hot	.082	—
CSN, Exports, Hot	.094	—
COSIPA, Exports, Cold	.039	—
CSN, Exports, Cold	.334	—
CSN, Exports, Tin	.019	—

levels for the original run (the same as the original run of the first experiment) and for the modified run. The results of the modified run should correspond roughly to the actual product flows in Brazil in 1964. Some of the flows were roughly the same as the actual flows. For example, there were shipments of plate from USIMINAS to Rio de Janeiro, of cold sheets and strip from COSIPA to São Paulo, and of tin plate from CSN to São Paulo.

The partial figures on USIMINAS production and exportation in 1965[5] point out some of the modifications that should be made in this and future models. First, pig iron production was substantially below the anticipation of the model. This may have resulted from the shipping bottleneck at the port of Vitoria which had not reached the expanded capacity required to ensure a smooth flow of products. Or the difference may have resulted from the decreased level of economic activity in Brazil in 1965 that resulted from an effort to slow the inflation. Or the overestimate of the model solution may have resulted from a failure to account for the operational difficulties inherent in the start-up of any new steel plant. Most likely the difference resulted from a combination of these and other factors not included in the model.

Second, the USIMINAS data show substantial exports of pig iron, ingot steel, slabs, and steel plate in 1964 — none of which were predicted by the model. This result showed the importance in further development of the model of including the possibility of the exportation of intermediate products such as pig iron, ingot steel, and slabs as well as that of final products. Such modifications were made in the expanded model discussed in the next chapter.

Capacity Addition

The cost of most capital equipment used in steel production is so great that many governments require government approval of all projects for any substantial investment requiring imported equipment. In other cases part of the financing of the investment comes from the government. In these instances there may at times be rival claims from several companies who want to expand their production facilities. Then the government may be faced with the problem of deciding between two or three plans. This experiment shows how a linear model may be used to provide a partial answer to this type of problem.

Here we consider the question of adding a new tinning line with a capacity of 200 thousand tons per year. A new tinning line is added to the capacity of each plant in turn to see where in the system it should be located to minimize total operating and transportation costs. (We assume that the capital cost of locating the new tin mill at each of the three steel mills would be the same, so that we need only consider the differences in operating and transportation costs.) All parameters in the model are the same as for the first test.

[5] ILAFA, *Revista latinoamericana de siderurgia* (monthly), Santiago, Chile, No. 59 (March 1965), p. 18.

The value of the objective function for the original solution before the addition of the new tinning line was $93.446 million. This amount was decreased by $270 thousand by locating the new line at COSIPA, by $136 thousand by placing it at CSN, and by $50 thousand by installing it at USIMINAS. Thus, a significant annual saving is gained from locating the new mill at the COSIPA plant.

Since the profitability of installing a new tinning line is apparently affected strongly by the availability of cold strip mill capacity, it would appear wise to make additional tests to consider the addition of a new tinning line together with an additional cold strip mill in each plant.

Transportation Cost

In Chapter 4 it was observed that there had been a secular decline in the dollar value of deflated railroad freight rates in Brazil over the period 1959 to 1963. In this test the parameters of the railroad transportation cost function were varied to see what the effects might have been on the steel industry of this decrease in railroad freight rates. It was assumed that truck freight rates decreased at the same rate as railroad freight rates.

In the railroad transportation cost function $T = a + bX + u$, we used values of 1.80 and 0.00700 for a and b, respectively, for most of the experiments with the model. Table 4.3 shows that the maximum value for the parameter a was 2.61 (1959) and the minimum value was 1.54 (1963). Similarly the maximum value for the parameter b was 0.00896 (1959) and 0.00644 (1963).

The values of the parameters a and b used in the experimental runs are shown in Table 5.7. Note that values used in the experiment have a range about twice that of the range observed between 1959 and 1963.

TABLE 5.7   VALUES OF THE PARAMETERS a AND b USED IN THE TRANSPORTATION COST TEST

Run	a	b
Original	1.80	0.00700
1	0.90	0.00350
2	1.35	0.00525
3	2.25	0.00875
4	2.70	0.01050

Table 5.8 shows that when the transportation cost was decreased from the original level there were some readjustments; however when the cost was increased there was no change in the activity levels. When the trans-

TABLE 5.8 TRANSPORTATION COST TEST: CHANGES IN ACTIVITY LEVELS
OF VARIABLES (*millions of metric tons*)

Activity	Original Run	Run 1	Run 2
COSIPA, São Paulo, Plate	.020		
COSIPA, Rio de Janeiro, Plate	—	+.054	+.054
USIMINAS, Rio de Janeiro, Plate	.160	−.054	−.054
USIMINAS, Belo Horizonte, Plate	.020		
COSIPA, São Paulo, Hot	.200		
USIMINAS, Rio de Janeiro, Hot	.064	+.056	+.056
USIMINAS, Belo Horizonte, Hot	.080		
CSN, Rio de Janeiro, Hot	.056	−.056	−.056
COSIPA, São Paulo, Cold	.300		
COSIPA, Rio de Janeiro, Cold	—	+.040	+.040
USIMINAS, Rio de Janeiro, Cold	.006		
USIMINAS, Belo Horizonte, Cold	.140		
CSN, Rio de Janeiro, Cold	.154	−.039	−.039
CSN, São Paulo, Tin	.150		
CSN, Rio de Janeiro, Tin	.060		
CSN, Belo Horizonte, Tin	.040		
COSIPA, Exports, Hot	.082	−.056	−.056
CSN, Exports, Hot	.094	+.056	+.056
COSIPA, Exports, Cold	.040	−.040	−.040
CSN, Exports, Cold	.335	+.040	+.040
CSN, Exports, Tin	.017		

portation cost decreased, CSN lost part of its nearby market in Rio de Janeiro to the more distant plants of COSIPA and USIMINAS.

Limitations of the Single-Period Model

The construction of an economic model is itself an optimizing problem where the objective is to approximate the reality with the strongest possible analytical tool and where this objective is constrained by (1) the rapidity of solution of the model, (2) the availability of data about the present, and (3) the uncertainty of projections for the future.

Rapidity of Solution

If rapidity of solution were not a constraint, one could simply write programs to consider all the possible combinations of events and then select from them the least-cost combination. However, this type of exercise is prohibitively expensive even for relatively small models such as the one presented here. With 66 possible activities to choose from (the

number of columns in the linear programming matrix) and with constraints and a matrix such that the rank of the matrix is 21 (the number
of activities in the solution), there are some $\binom{66}{21} = 9.05 \times 10^{16}$ possible extreme solutions. A linear programming algorithm is simply a way
of beginning with one of these extreme solutions and considering only a
small subset of them in arriving at an optimum solution.

So when a problem can be structured so as to approximate closely
the nonlinearities in the system with linear functions and at the same
time to fit the other requirements of a linear programming problem, one
can take advantage of this powerful computational method. Various
types of nonlinear programming models offer better approximations to
the nonlinear parts of the system but sacrifice computational efficiency.
Thus, one is faced with a choice of using a nonlinear model that gives a
closer fit to a part of the reality but that limits very sharply the number
of plants, markets, and products which can be included in the model or
of using a linear model with more plants, markets, and products but
with a poorer approximation to the nonlinear parts of the system. For
this part of the study a linear model has been used; for the next part a
nonlinear model will be used.

What then is the extent of the cost of using a linear rather than a nonlinear model? Linear programming models require that all costs be
linear functions of their activity levels or use. As has been discussed
earlier, this is not a restrictive assumption for raw material cost but is a
violation of the reality of labor cost.

Labor cost is a nonlinear function of the level of production in that a
certain number of men are needed to operate and maintain the productive units whether they are used to capacity or not. Also, in most
steel mills the firms are constrained by strong unions from laying off
and adding to the labor force in the plant at will. However, the nonlinearities in labor cost would not appear to cause a significant bias in
the results because the component of labor cost in total cost is small.

The linearity of the model also requires that the cost of each activity
be independent of the level of all other activities. This problem was mentioned earlier. The assumption would seem to be valid for independence
in the cost of activities in different plants or in the cost of importing and
exporting activities; however, it is less valid for independence among the
activities within a given plant.

Even when using a linear programming model the rapidity of solution
sharply constrains the number of products, markets, and plants that can
be considered in a problem. Since it was desirable to have a model that
could be solved in five to ten minutes on the IBM 1620 (a small com-

puter), the problem was limited to four products, three market areas, and three plants. As was mentioned earlier, the limitation to four products prevented the model from catching in its analytical net many important distinctions. For example, the differentiation between heavy and light, narrow and wide steel plates is not considered. Likewise, there is no consideration in the model of the quality or width of hot and cold rolled sheets and strips. Also, the problem has been limited to a consideration of only flat steel products.

The limitation to three market areas prevents consideration of the fact that a portion of the requirement for steel products is located in parts of the country distant from the southern triangle of São Paulo, Rio de Janeiro, and Belo Horizonte. However, in the case of flat steel products, which are used almost entirely as intermediate products for manufacturing other goods, the assumption of point concentration of markets in this area provides a close approximation to reality.

In limiting the analysis to three plants we excluded from consideration a number of other plants that produced flat products. However, aside from the firm Belgo-Mineria which was producing about 100 thousand tons of flat products a year, none of the excluded plants was a large-volume producer of flat steel products.

The desire for rapidity of solution of the problem also limited the ability to consider scheduling problems or fluctuations in requirements and output over the course of a year. The model permitted no consideration of the fact that during a certain part of the year a consumer of steel products might be willing to pay a premium in order to have the products available sooner. Likewise, transportation bottlenecks might have prevented the smooth flow of products over the course of a year.

Availability of Data

The treatment of transportation cost in this volume provides a good example of the limitations placed on this type of study by the availability of data. Ideally the information that would be used is the real social cost of transporting the products. These real social costs should reflect capacity constraints as well as other variables. Since that type of information is not available, one may resort to the rates actually charged to each steel company for shipment of each product over a wide variety of routes via three or four different means of transportation. If that is not available, one may approximate these costs by using published data for railroad rates for steel products and estimating the functions described in an earlier section of this chapter.

One of the most serious data constraints on the model is the lack of a detailed breakdown, by type of product, market area, and year, of consumption of flat steel products.

Uncertainty

Neither this model nor the mixed-integer programming model discussed in the following chapters deals with the problem of uncertainty except in a very limited fashion. Considering the limited time available for preparing the study it was decided to concentrate first on the preparation of the mixed-integer programming model under certainty and to postpone the added complication of uncertainty.

Uncertainty can be dealt with in this type of model by varying the parameters of the model within expected limits and running the model repeatedly with these changes. The tests described for changes in transportation and other cost parameters and for changes in requirement levels are of this type. The facility with which the original elements of the matrix can be stored on disks or magnetic tape, and then modified one at a time or in groups without the necessity of reloading the entire matrix for each run, is a great aid in conducting this type of test.

A more systematic treatment of uncertainty may be made through the use of a modification of linear programming called "chance constrained programming." [6]

[6] See A. Charnes and W. W. Cooper, "Chance Constrained Programming," *Management Science,* Vol. 6 (October 1959), pp. 73–80; and an application of this technique to transportation investment planning by Pedro N. Taborga, "Determination of an Optimal System of Transportation for Chile," mimeo., Department of Civil Engineering, Massachusetts Institute of Technology, January 1965.

6

Description of the Multiperiod Model

This chapter presents an application of the multiperiod model to the problem of when and where to add to capacity in an existing system of steel plants. This multi-time-period model uses an expanded version of the linear programming model of the previous chapter as the submodel for each time period. An investment matrix is appended to the multi-time-period model, and additional rows are added to the bottom of the matrix to constrain the investment variables to take on only the values of zero or one. Thus, with the transportation-production activities of each time period free to take on any nonnegative value, and the investment activities constrained to zero or one integer values, the model becomes a mixed-integer programming model.

The expanded version of the linear programming model that is the submodel for each time period permits the shipment between plants of the three intermediate products (pig iron, ingot steel, and slabs) instead of the single intermediate product (ingot steel) of the previous model. Also, the enlarged version of the model permits the importation and exportation of each of the three intermediate products. As there is a substantial trade in intermediate products in the steel industry, this addition to the model enhances its approximation to reality.

In the single-period model, the blast furnace and steel shop were treated as a single productive unit. In the new version these two processes are treated as separate productive units.

Twenty-three possible investment projects were singled out for consideration. The investment matrix consists of a separate activity for each of twenty-three investment opportunities. These each refer to a specific size, location, time period, and process stage. More candidate projects could have been listed but were omitted in order to economize on computations. Four of the investment opportunities are for projects that could be completed by the beginning of the second time period, seven are for projects that could be completed for the third time period, and the remaining twelve are for projects that could be completed for the fourth time period. Thus, the problem of the model is one of choosing that combination of investment projects, domestic production, exports, and imports that minimizes the present value of the cost of meeting the product requirements in all market areas during the period July 1, 1967, to January 1, 1975.

The notation of the model was set up for a ten-year span consisting of four time periods, each of two and a half years duration. However, the first time period of January 1, 1965, to July 1, 1967, was excluded from the model because investment decisions made in 1965 would not affect the structure of the industry until 1967. Therefore, the model includes period 2 (July 1, 1967, to January 1, 1970); period 3 (January 1, 1970, to July 1, 1972); and period 4 (July 1, 1972, to January 1, 1975).

The form of this and the next chapter parallels that of the previous two chapters. This chapter contains a discussion of the data inputs to the model, and in Chapter 7 the computational methods are explained and the results analyzed. The primary difference between this chapter and Chapter 5, which described the data inputs to the linear programming problem, is that here a discussion of the component parts of the matrix and the right-hand side of the problem is to be used as the vehicle for carrying the discussion of the data used in the model.

Elements of the Matrix and the Right-Hand Side

A discussion of the structure of the multiperiod model matrix and the right-hand side is given in Appendix F. The parameters for the right-hand side are presented in the appendix but their derivation is discussed later in this chapter.

The Coefficients in the Objective Function

Discounting of the Cost for Production-Transportation Activities

The coefficients in the objective function are the present values of the costs of operating each of the activities of the model at the unit level. These coefficients were calculated in three steps. First, the cost was calculated of producing and transporting a product, or exporting or importing it at a rate of one metric ton per year. Second, a discount factor was calculated for the production-transportation activities of each time period to discount all cost back to January 1, 1965, as follows:

R = discount rate per six-month period.

D_t = discount factor for the production-transportation cost incurred in time period t.

$$D_t = \frac{1}{(1+R)^{5(t-1)+1}} + \frac{1}{(1+R)^{5(t-1)+2}} + \cdots + \frac{1}{(1+R)^{5(t-1)+5}} \quad (6.1)$$

Each time period is made up of two and one-half years or five six-month periods; therefore it is necessary to generate a discount factor for periods that are not annual. Function 6.1 adds up the five components of the discount factor of each time period. Thus the components for period 2 are the sixth through tenth six-month periods.

It is assumed that all activities operate at a constant level *within* any single time period; that is, the level of activities changes only at the end of each two-and-a-half-year period. Also, it is assumed that the discount rate R does not change over time. This assumption could be modified easily if projections of the discount rate over time were available.

Third, the activity cost per year is divided in half. This gives the cost of operating the activity at that level for six months instead of for one year. Then the discount factor is applied to give the present value of the cost of operating the activity over the two and a half years covered by the time period in which the activity takes place.

For example, the cost of producing a ton of steel plate at the COSIPA plant is calculated to be \$57.95 and the transportation cost from COSIPA to São Paulo is calculated to be \$2.66. Therefore, the activity cost for the production of one metric ton of steel plate at COSIPA and its shipment to São Paulo is \$60.61. Then, the cost of supplying steel plate for six months at an annual rate of one million metric tons per year to the São Paulo market area from the COSIPA plant would be \$30.30 million. The present value of the cost of this activity in the second time period (assuming a discount rate of 5 per cent per six months or 10 per cent per year) would then be

$$C' = \$30.3 \left(\frac{1}{(1+.05)^6} + \frac{1}{(1+.05)^7} + \cdots + \frac{1}{(1+.05)^{10}} \right)$$

$$C' = (\$30.3)(.746 + .711 + .677 + .645 + .614)$$

$$C' = (\$30.3)(3.393)$$

$$C' = \$102.80 \text{ million per million metric tons}$$

= the present value of the cost of the activity.

The method of discounting for the activity cost of the investment opportunities was somewhat different and will be discussed separately later. The method of discounting just described was used for all production-transportation activities, including the trade in intermediate products and the importation and exportation of all intermediate and final products. With an annual discount rate of 10 per cent, the discount factors for the three time periods were

$$D_2 = 3.393$$
$$D_3 = 2.658$$
$$D_4 = 2.083.$$

Cost Calculation for the Production-Transportation Activities

For the single-period model of the previous chapters detailed cost calculations were made for the cost of pig iron and ingot steel at each plant. Then the costs of other products were approximated, depending upon the amount of ingot steel required to fabricate the final product, as a constant multiplied by the cost of ingot steel. For the multiperiod model the detailed cost calculations made for pig iron and ingot steel at each plant were extended to include a detailed production cost of slabs, steel plate, hot sheet and strip, cold sheet and strip, and tin plate.

A study was made at the Volta Redonda plant of CSN in 1962 to determine the scrap credit and the conversion cost at each step in the process of producing flat steel products.[1] The results of that study have been used in this chapter as the basis for the cost calculations for rolled products for the multiperiod model. Since the 1962 study did not give a breakdown of conversion cost into its component parts and since data on conversion cost for final products in the other two plants were not made available, the conversion cost in all three plants was assumed to be the same. This assumption would appear to introduce some bias in favor of CSN because the two newer plants would be expected to be capable of producing with a lower conversion cost.

Since scrap prices differ significantly at the three plants, separate estimates were made for the scrap credits at each stage in the process at each plant. This was accomplished by using the specific consumption data from CSN and multiplying the coefficient for the amount of scrap generated by the value of scrap at the plant concerned. Table 6.1 gives the results of these calculations, as well as the conversion cost at each step.

The costs of pig iron and ingot steel at each plant were calculated as described in Chapter 4. The cost of the product leaving each of the thirteen productive units listed in Table 6.1 is calculated by multiplying

---

[1] The scrap credit is the value of the scrap generated at each point in the production process. The conversion cost is the labor, energy, and material costs of processing the product at each production unit. Though a breakdown of the component parts of conversion cost was not available, it was noted that about $17 of the conversion cost of $24.93 for electrolytic tin was due to the tin cost.

the specific consumption by the cost per metric ton of the product leaving the previous productive unit in the line, subtracting scrap credit, and adding the conversion cost. The results of these calculations are shown in Table 6.2 and in greater detail in Appendix D.[2]

TABLE 6.1   SCRAP CREDIT AND CONVERSION COST FOR FLAT STEEL PRODUCTS*

Process	Specific Consumption Product	Scrap Credit (U.S. dollars per metric ton)			Conversion Cost (U.S. dollars per metric ton)
		COSIPA	USIMINAS	CSN	
Primary mill	1.090	2.25	3.15	2.34	2.81
Scarfing	1.000	—	—	—	1.03
Reheating	1.000	—	—	—	2.56
Roughing mill	1.028	.70	.98	.73	2.46
Hot strip mill	1.013	.32	.45	.34	3.62
Pickling line	1.068	1.70	2.38	1.77	2.39
Cold strip mill	1.005	.12	.17	.13	5.79
Electrolytic cleaning	1.017	.42	.59	.44	2.18
Annealing	1.000	—	—	—	2.13
Temper mill	1.014	.35	.49	.36	2.83
Cleaning of coils	1.071	1.77	2.48	1.85	.77
Electrolytic tinning	.996	—	—	—	24.93
Inspection and packaging	1.000	—	—	—	14.04

* The costs shown in this table are based on a study of the Volta Redonda plant of Companhia Siderurgica Nacional in 1962. The free market exchange rate of 359 cruzeiros = U.S. $1.00 that existed in May 1962 was used to convert from cruzeiro cost to dollar cost.

Since capital cost on all installed equipment is treated as sunk cost and therefore beyond the control of the decision makers, it is excluded from these estimates. The cost of working capital is also excluded but it should not be.

A change was made in the method of calculating the transportation cost for shipping *intermediate* products between plants. In the previous

[2] The cost of pig iron and ingot steel at the three plants is slightly different in this table from the cost shown in the previous chapter. This is due to a change in the specific consumption of water in the production of pig iron at COSIPA from .650 to .065. Similarly, there is a change in the specific consumption of electrical energy in the production of pig iron at COSIPA from .007 to .070, and a change in the specific consumption of blast furnace gas at USIMINAS from −2.624 to −3.300 and at CSN from −2.624 to −3.715.

TABLE 6.2 PRODUCTION COST
(*U.S. dollars per metric ton*)

Plant	Pig Iron	Ingots	Slabs	Plate	Hot Strip	Cold Strip	Tin Plate
COSIPA	31.97	46.34	51.07	57.95	62.00	72.91	125.02
USIMINAS	29.47	42.80	46.32	52.78	56.63	66.41	116.84
CSN	36.52	49.84	54.80	61.75	65.84	76.95	129.37

model these costs were estimated from the transportation costs for final products over certain routes. Now they are calculated as follows:

$$\bar{T} = .7(a + bX) \tag{6.2}$$

where $\bar{T}$ is the transportation cost per metric ton over the distance X between plants and the parameters a and b are as estimated in Chapter 4. The resulting transportation cost for shipping intermediate products between plants is as follows:

From	To	Cost (U.S. dollars per metric ton
COSIPA	USIMINAS	7.63
COSIPA	CSN	3.37
USIMINAS	CSN	5.51

The rates both to and from a given pair of plants are assumed to be the same: there are no back haul rates.

Objective Function Coefficients for Intermediate Products Shipments

The activity cost for all production-transportation activities delivering final products to market areas includes the cost of producing the pig iron, ingot steel, and slabs required to manufacture the final product. Therefore, when a plant receives shipments of one of the intermediate products from another plant, it is necessary to subtract the costs of producing the products in the receiving plant from the costs of producing the goods in the shipping plant and transporting them to the receiving plant. For example, the activity cost of COSIPA–São Paulo plate includes the total cost of manufacturing a metric ton of steel plate at COSIPA and shipping it to São Paulo; that is, it includes the cost of producing the pig iron, ingot steel, slabs, and so on. If COSIPA receives a part of its pig iron from USIMINAS there would be double accounting if the cost of producing that amount of pig iron at COSIPA were not subtracted out. Therefore, in calculating the activity cost for USIMINAS-COSIPA pig iron it is necessary to add together the cost of producing the pig iron at USIMINAS and the cost of shipping it from that plant to COSIPA and then subtract from the sum the cost of producing a ton of pig iron at COSIPA. Thus, the cost for these activities, the coefficients a_{il}^{kt}, is the extra cost to the system of producing the intermediate product k in plant i and shipping it to plant l. Of course, this activity cost may be a negative number in cases where the difference in the cost of raw materials at the two plants is so large that the transportation cost between the plants is not sufficient to absorb the difference.

TABLE 6.3   ACTIVITY COST FOR INTERMEDIATE PRODUCT SHIPMENT ACTIVITIES
(*U.S. dollars per metric ton*)

Activity	Time Period			Activity Cost
	2nd	3rd	4th	
COSIPA, USIMINAS				
Pig iron	17.18	13.46	10.55	10.12
Steel	18.94	14.84	11.63	11.19
Slab	21.01	16.46	12.90	12.41
COSIPA, CSN				
Pig iron	−2.02	−1.58	−1.24	−1.19
Steel	−.22	−.18	−.14	−.13
Slab	−.61	−.47	−.37	−.36
USIMINAS, COSIPA				
Pig iron	8.70	6.82	5.34	5.13
Steel	6.94	5.44	4.26	4.10
Slab	4.87	3.82	2.99	2.88
USIMINAS, CSN				
Pig iron	−2.61	−2.05	−1.60	−1.54
Steel	−2.58	−2.02	−1.59	−1.52
Slab	−5.03	−3.94	−3.09	−2.97
CSN, COSIPA				
Pig iron	13.44	10.53	8.25	7.94
Steel	11.65	9.12	7.15	6.88
Slab	12.03	9.42	7.38	7.11
CSN, USIMINAS				
Pig iron	21.32	16.70	13.09	12.58
Steel	21.29	16.68	13.07	12.57
Slab	23.73	18.60	14.57	14.00

Even when the activity cost for an intermediate-product shipment activity takes on a negative value, the capacity constraints and the necessity of filling the requirements of the market areas, plus the fact that all exports also have negative activity cost, may cause the activity to be at the zero level in the solution. Rather, these intermediate-product shipment activities are used when there is an imbalance in the capacity structure of two plants in their basic production units. Thus, if one plant has an excess of steelmaking capacity (relative to the capacity of its primary mill) and a second plant has a large primary mill but insufficient steelmaking capacity, then the activity will be chosen if it is more profitable to the system than the export of excess ingot steel from the original plant and/or the import of ingot steel to the second plant.

Table 6.3 shows the activity cost for each of the intermediate-product shipping activities in each of the time periods. The first three columns of the table give the present value of the cost of performing the activity at a level of one metric ton per year over the two and a half years of the time period. The fourth column gives a reference for comparison with the previous model, a number that is easier to compare to prices — the undiscounted annual activity cost in U.S. dollars per metric ton.

This table shows that under the assumptions of the model and *independent of capital cost* both COSIPA and USIMINAS can supply the intermediate products to CSN less expensively than these can be produced at CSN. However, as was already noted, this is not to say that they *should* supply intermediate products to CSN because the total cost to the system may be less if the capacity in the basic production units, that is, the blast furnace, steel shop, and primary mill, at COSIPA and USIMINAS is used to meet their own requirements for intermediate products.

Objective Function Coefficients for Imported Intermediate Products

The annual undiscounted cost for these activities, the coefficients b_i^{kt}, were calculated (1) by using Pittsburgh prices for pig iron, ingot steel, and slabs,[3] (2) adding intercontinental transportation cost by ship, (3) adding transportation cost from the port to the plant, and (4) subtracting the cost of producing the intermediate product in the importing plant. Step (4) is necessary for the same reason that it is necessary in calculating the activity cost for the production and transportation of intermediate products between plants. This procedure yields an estimate of the added cost to the system of importing the intermediate product concerned rather than of producing it domestically.

Pittsburgh prices for May 12, 1965, were obtained in dollars per ton and converted to dollars per metric ton to give the following prices:[4]

---

[3] Since Brazil receives steel imports from a number of countries, Pittsburgh prices are used here only as representative. A better procedure would be to use projections of the prices for the marginal source of the imports of each product.
[4] *Steel*, Vol. 158 (May 17, 1965), p. 68.

	U.S. Dollars per Metric Ton
Pig iron	70.50
Ingots	88.30
Slabs	92.50

The transportation cost used was $15.00 per metric ton. This estimate was based on one used in the TECHINT study for the Propulsora plant in Argentina for the transportation cost from the Benelux countries to Buenos Aires.[5]

The transportation cost from the port to the plant was assumed to be zero at COSIPA since the plant is right on the water's edge; it was assumed to be $3 per metric ton for USIMINAS and CSN.

Activity Costs for Production-Transportation Activities for Final Products

These activity costs c_{ij}^k were calculated by adding the production costs at plant i (see Table 6.2) to the transportation costs for final product k from plant i to market area j (Table 6.4). The transportation costs were estimated as discussed in Chapter 4.

TABLE 6.4 TRANSPORTATION COST

Plant	Market Area	Cost (U.S. dollars per metric ton)
COSIPA	São Paulo	2.66
COSIPA	Rio de Janeiro	6.37
COSIPA	Belo Horizonte	8.16
USIMINAS	São Paulo	7.72
USIMINAS	Rio de Janeiro	6.28
USIMINAS	Belo Horizonte	3.30
CSN	São Paulo	4.27
CSN	Rio de Janeiro	2.94
CSN	Belo Horizonte	5.11

For tables of distances between plants, and between plants and markets, as well as tables of specific inputs, costs of inputs, and cost breakdowns for pig iron and ingot steel in each of the three plants, see Appendix D.

Activity Costs of Importation of Final Products

These activity costs d_i^{kt} were calculated (1) by taking Pittsburgh prices of the products, (2) adding transportation cost to Brazilian ports,

[5] "Proyecto de un establecimiento siderúrgica a ciclo integral," by TECHINT, Buenos Aires, for Propulsora Siderúrgica (Milano, Italy, October 1964).

and (3) adding a sum for the cost of transportation from the port to the market area.

The Pittsburgh prices in dollars per metric ton as of May 12, 1965, were as follows:[6]

	U.S. Dollars per Metric Ton
Plates	122
Hot-rolled sheets	117
Cold-rolled sheets	144
Tin plate, electroplate	201

The transportation cost was assumed to be $15 per metric ton and the cost from the ports to the market areas was assumed to be zero for Rio de Janeiro, $2 per metric ton for São Paulo, and $8 per metric ton for Belo Horizonte.

Activity Costs of Exportation of Intermediate and Final Products

The profits $\hat{e}^{kt}$ from export activities were calculated by taking the difference between the cost of production plus transportation to the nearest port and the f.o.b. price for Brazilian exports in 1964.[7] Table 6.5 shows the quantity, value, and unit value of these exports.[8]

The transportation cost between the plants and ports for exporting activities is assumed to be $3 per metric ton for the CSN and USIMINAS plants and $1 per metric ton for the COSIPA plant.

Table 6.6 shows the resulting assumptions as to Brazilian f.o.b. prices in comparison with selected U.S. and Japanese prices. Since steel prices

[6] *Steel*, Vol. 158 (May 17, 1965), p. 68.

[7] The results of this study indicate that exports play a large enough role in the Brazilian steel industry that careful projections of export prices should be made for incorporation into this type of model. Also, the exporting activities should be constrained or set up with linear segments to exhibit decreasing returns if the detailed export studies indicate that diminishing returns on exports exist for the Brazilian steel industry within the relevant ranges.

[8] Since hot and cold sheets were included in the same category but divided between thick and thin sheets, an aggregate price was first obtained by weighting the unit price of the thick and thin sheets by the amount of each exported and then dividing by the total amount exported. This yielded an aggregate export price for hot and cold sheets of $128.82. Observing that the difference between the prices of hot and cold sheet in Pittsburgh was about $27 per metric ton, the amount of $13.50 per metric ton was subtracted from and added to $128.82 to obtain prices of $115.32 and $142.32 for hot and cold sheet and strip, respectively.

The amount of tin plate exported was so little and the price so far from U.S. prices that it was decided to put the f.o.b. price for tin plate at $10 under the Pittsburgh price, that is, at $191 per metric ton.

TABLE 6.5 BRAZILIAN EXPORTS OF SELECTED STEEL PRODUCTS IN 1964

Product	Quantity* (thousands of metric tons)	Value* (thousands of U.S. dollars)	F.O.B. Unit Value (U.S. dollars per metric ton)
Pig iron	148.9	5,184.0	34.80
Ingots	10.2	360.0	35.30
Slabs, blooms, etc.	38.6	3,115.0	80.60
Plates	12.4	1,344.0	108.30
Hot and cold sheets between 3mm and 4.75mm	7.9	1,043.0	131.90
Hot and cold sheets less than 3mm	2.0	233.0	116.50
Tin plate	.012	1.3	109.20

*From *Revista latinoamericana de siderurgia*, published by the Instituto Latinoamericano del Fierro y el Acero, Santiago, Chile, No. 62 (June 1965), p. 24.

differ with different sizes, shapes, and qualities of products and the results shown in the table are also sensitive to the choice of exchange rate, the comparison is very rough. However, it would appear that the assumptions used in the model underestimate the price that the Brazilian

TABLE 6.6 COMPARISON OF BRAZILIAN F.O.B. PRICES WITH JAPANESE AND U.S. PRICES (*U.S. dollars per metric ton*)

	Brazilian F.O.B. Prices, 1964	Japanese, 1965*	U.S.– Pittsburgh, 1965†	U.S.– Birmingham, 1965*
Pig iron	34.80		70.50	65.00
Ingots	35.30		88.30	
Slabs	80.60		92.50	
Plates	108.30	102.78	122.00	
Hot strip	115.32		117.00	
Cold strip	142.32	125.00	144.00	
Tin plate	191.00		201.00	

*From *Steel*, May 17, 1965, p. 74.
†From *Steel*, May 17, 1965, p. 68.

steel companies could obtain for exports of pig iron and ingot steel. In fact, Table 6.7 shows that in the short run the system, once the capital is installed, would receive very small gains from the exportation of pig iron and no gains at all from the exportation of ingot steel. On the other hand, it shows that the system could make large gains from exporting slabs, plates, hot strip, cold strip, and tin plate. However, in the long

TABLE 6.7 CALCULATION OF UNDISCOUNTED ANNUAL ACTIVITY COST
FOR EXPORT ACTIVITIES (*U.S. dollars per metric ton*)

Export Activities	F.O.B. Unit Value	Production Cost* Plus Transportation Cost to Port	Undiscounted Annual Activity Cost
COSIPA			
Pig iron	34.80	32.97	−1.83
Steel	35.30	47.34	12.04
Slabs	80.60	52.07	−28.53
Plate	108.30	58.95	−49.35
Hot	115.32	63.00	−52.32
Cold	142.32	73.91	−68.41
Tin	191.00	126.02	−64.98
USIMINAS			
Pig iron	34.80	32.47	−2.33
Steel	35.30	45.80	10.50
Slabs	80.60	49.32	−31.28
Plate	108.30	55.78	−52.52
Hot	115.32	59.63	−55.69
Cold	142.32	69.41	−72.91
Tin	191.00	119.84	−71.16
CSN			
Pig iron	34.80	39.52	4.72
Steel	35.30	52.84	17.54
Slabs	80.60	57.80	−22.80
Plate	108.30	64.75	−43.55
Hot	115.32	68.84	−46.48
Cold	142.32	79.95	−62.37
Tin	191.00	132.37	−58.63

* "Production cost" here does not include capital cost.

run, the system weighs both the gains from exporting and the necessity of meeting domestic requirements in deciding when and where to add additional capacity.

There is a certain level of export profits at which it would be desirable to import the domestic requirements and to export domestic production and/or to install all the new capacity possible in order to reap the large profits from exporting. However, even though the author has little confidence in the data inputs to the model on import prices and export profits, the conclusions of the model roughly approximate a reasonable estimation of how this part of the Brazilian steel industry may be expected to perform during the decade 1965–1975.

The international trade assumptions implicit in this model are that the government of Brazil is in a position to control all exports and imports of flat steel products, that the government wants to minimize the total use of Brazilian resources to satisfy the steel requirements of the country, and that export "profits" to the system are, in the short run, the difference between f.o.b. prices and the cost (with capital cost excluded) of producing the products and loading them on ships. With this sort of a model, if there is excess capacity in any of the productive units after the domestic requirements have been satisfied, there is an incentive for the country to sell its excess abroad so long as the price to be obtained for it is above the cost (with capital cost excluded) of production and transportation cost to the port (including loading cost). Thus a practice that is called "dumping" (that is, one country sells its excess in another country at a price below the domestic price plus transportation charges between countries) is permitted in the model. Decisions on whether or not to install new capacity are made on the basis of minimizing total cost less export credits in the system over time. In the short run, exports will be made whenever excess capacity is available and foreign prices are above marginal production cost plus transportation cost. In the long run, capacity will be installed for exporting activities provided the revenue to be gained from such enterprise is sufficient to cover the capital cost of the equipment and the production and transportation cost.[9]

Activity Costs of Investment Opportunities

The method used in calculating these costs f_r is discussed in the following section on the treatment of investment decisions in the model.

Treatment of Investment in the Model

If investment costs per ton of product were not a decreasing function of the size of the productive unit (between certain limits prescribed by the existing technology) but were, rather, a linear function of the size of the productive unit, then investment activities could be treated like any other activity of the model. However, the technological reality of the steel industry is not only that investment costs are characterized by economies of scale between certain size limits but also that many investment decisions are discrete: the problem is to decide when and where to install a new productive unit of a standard size that has been determined by other considerations.

For example, the steel shops at the USIMINAS and COSIPA plants both consist of a pair of LD converters. Since it is necessary to reline these converters once every two or three weeks (an operation that takes sev-

[9] Care must be taken in using linear economic models on this kind of problem. In the absence of the appropriate constraints, or the introduction of diminishing returns, solutions to this type of model may exhibit infinite profits and exports.

eral days to complete) and since it is desirable to maintain a steady flow of product through the plant, only one converter is maintained in operation at a time. Therefore, the effective capacity of the steel shops of these two plants is equivalent to that of a single converter which could be maintained in continuous operation without the necessity of relining the vessel.

When additional capacity is required in the steel shops of these plants, a third converter of the same size as the first two will be installed. Then two converters will be maintained in operation at a time while the third converter is being relined. Thus, for less than half the cost of the original investment in the steel shop, the companies will be able to double the effective capacity of this part of their plants. So the short-run question facing the investment planner in the Brazilian steel companies, in the case of these particular units, is not one of what size of converter to install but rather of when and where to install the new converter(s).

A similar situation arises for investments in some rolling mills. The roughing mill presently installed at the COSIPA plant is a reversing rougher. However, the plant was constructed so that at a later date additional roughing mills could be installed to convert the reversing rougher to a continuous rougher. Here once again the question facing the investment planner is not one of size but rather of when to make the installation of the additional capacity.

A third example is presented by the blast furnaces of COSIPA and USIMINAS. Both blast furnaces were installed without fuel injection, so it can be anticipated that when additional capacity is desired in either of these furnaces this modification will be made. The amount of oil injection will not be at issue as much as the appropriate time to install the modification.

For other investments, scale is a factor of major importance. For example, when a new blast furnace is installed at CSN, the company officials will be able (within certain limits) to buy any size of blast furnace they desire.

So it seems useful for investment planning models to consider the questions both of when and where to make additions to capacity and of what size of unit to install. The investigation described in this study has focused on the question of when and where to install units of given capacity. However, the method used here could be adapted easily to study the problem of investments under economies of scale. This could be done by providing the model with projects for units of various sizes at the same plant in the same time period and letting the model choose the desired size.

Also, it would be useful to explore the utilization of models in which investments in the near future (which are constrained by the technological situation of the existing productive units) would be assigned integer variables and projects for the more distant future would be assigned continuous variables, within certain bounds.

Selection of Investment Opportunities or Projects

The model most appropriate for considering the location of discrete additions to capacity is a model of the mixed-integer type. This class of mathematical programming models is not difficult to formulate but is very difficult to solve when a large number of integer variables are used. Even with advances in computation speeds and an algorithm employing a successful search technique, mixed-integer problems with more than twenty or thirty integer variables remain expensive to solve.

This limitation of the number of integer variables makes it necessary to formulate the problem carefully before attempting to solve it. Thus, as a preliminary to specification of the model, projections up to 1975 of requirements for flat steel products in Brazil were compared to the capacity presently installed in the major productive units in each of the three plants. These rough calculations, plus the experience from the single-period model described in the previous chapters, gave an indication of where the bottlenecks in the system would be in 1967, or 1970, or 1972. Also, the expansion plans of the three companies were reviewed and estimates were made of the time required to complete various projects for additions to capacity.

As a result of this exercise some twenty-three "investment opportunities" were chosen to include in the model. Table 6.8 gives a listing of these projects, the number of metric tons they would add to present capacity, the cost of the project, the gestation time for the project, and the expected life of the equipment once it is installed.

Relatively few projects were considered for the second time period because the existing capacity was sufficient (under the assumptions of the model) to serve most of the requirements and because the time between January 1965 and July 1967 was not sufficient to carry out a large project.

The four projects considered for the second time period were (1) the installation of a third LD converter, of an annual capacity of 800 thousand metric tons, at COSIPA, (2) the installation of a third LD converter of the same size at USIMINAS, (3) the addition of a tinning line with a capacity of 180 thousand metric tons per year to the rolling mill section of the COSIPA plant, and (4) the addition of a tinning line of the same size to the plant at CSN. So the problem for this time period was to decide whether to install a third LD converter at COSIPA or at USIMINAS, at both, or at neither—the converters to be in operation by

TABLE 6.8 INVESTMENT OPPORTUNITIES

Plant	Time Period	Productive Unit*	Addition to Capacity (million metric tons)	Cost (millions of U.S. dollars)	Gestation Time (years)	Life of Equipment (years)
COSIPA	2	3rd LD converter	.80	7.90	2	18
USIMINAS	2	3rd LD converter	.80	7.90	2	18
COSIPA	2	Tinning line	.18	8.00	2	20
CSN	2	Tinning line	.18	8.00	2	20
COSIPA	3	Blast furnace modifications	.28	1.80	1	20
USIMINAS	3	Blast furnace modifications	.36	2.40	1	20
COSIPA	3	3rd LD converter	.80	7.90	2	18
USIMINAS	3	3rd LD converter	.80	7.90	2	18
CSN	3	1st and 2nd LD converters	1.00	34.50	4	18
COSIPA	3	Tinning line	.18	8.00	2	20
CSN	3	Tinning line	.18	8.00	2	20
COSIPA	4	Blast furnace	.80	28.00	4	20
USIMINAS	4	Blast furnace	.80	28.00	4	20
CSN	4	Blast furnace	.80	28.00	4	20
COSIPA	4	4th and 5th LD converters	.80	23.60	4	18
USIMINAS	4	4th and 5th LD converters	.80	23.60	4	18
CSN	4	1st and 2nd LD converters	1.00	34.50	4	18
COSIPA	4	Added stand for roughing mill	1.00	25.00	3	20
COSIPA	4	Cold strip mill	.35	10.00	2	20
USIMINAS	4	Cold strip mill	.35	10.00	2	20
CSN	4	Cold strip mill	.35	10.00	2	20
COSIPA	4	Tinning line	.18	8.00	2	20
CSN	4	Tinning line	.18	8.00	2	20

* LD converters are Linz-Donawitz oxygen converters.

July 1, 1967. Also, it was necessary to decide whether to install a new tinning line at COSIPA or at CSN, at both, or at neither.

Seven investment possibilities were considered for the third time period. Two of these were for investments in blast furnaces, three were for investments in steel shops, and two were for investments in tinning lines. The first project was for the installation of petroleum injection in the blast furnace at COSIPA. It was estimated that this would add 280 thousand metric tons per year to the existing 800 thousand metric tons per year capacity of the furnace. The second investment was for the installation of fuel injection in the two blast furnaces at the USIMINAS plant. This investment, it was assumed, would add 300 thousand metric tons per year to the capacity of these furnaces.[10]

The third and fourth investments in the third time period were identical to the projects for addition of a third LD converter to the steel shops at COSIPA and USIMINAS in the second time period. Since it is the usual practice to add a third converter and then to add a fourth and fifth as a pair, the model should have been constrained to prevent investment in a third LD converter at COSIPA in both the second and in the third time periods.

The fifth investment in this time period is for the installation of a pair of LD converters at CSN. The existing steel shop at CSN consisted of eight open-hearth furnaces, but it was assumed that when additional capacity was installed in the steel shop at this plant it would be in the form of a pair of LD converters.

The last two projects for this period were identical to the two investments in tinning lines in the second time period. The constraint to prevent the installation of a tinning line at COSIPA or at CSN in both time periods was not necessary because the cost of an additional tinning line is relatively independent of the number of tinning lines already installed at a particular plant.

There were twelve projects that could be completed by the beginning of the fourth time period in July of 1972. The first three of these projects were for the installation of blast furnaces with annual capacities of 800 thousand metric tons at each of the three plants. The next two projects were for the installation of a pair of LD converters at COSIPA and/or at USIMINAS. It was assumed that the model would choose to install a third LD converter at each of the plants for either the second or third time period so that further increments to capacity in the steel shops of these plants for the fourth time period would require the addition of new pairs of LD converters.

The next investment project, that is, for a first and second LD converter at CSN, is identical to the investment for the previous time period in the steel shop at CSN. The next project in the list is for the installation of an additional stand in the roughing mill at COSIPA. This mill was referred to earlier in a discussion of the discrete nature of many investments in the steel industry in the short run. The investment would have converted the mill from a reversing to a continuous mill, and it

---

[10] These estimates of the increase in capacity that could result from fuel injection were at best guesses and were based in a rough way on the experience of the blast furnace of the Chilean steel company, CAP.

was estimated that the investment would increase the capacity of the existing unit from one million metric tons per year to two million metric tons per year.

Projects for the installation of new cold strip mills at COSIPA, USIMINAS, and CSN follow. Each of these mills would have had a capacity of 350 thousand metric tons per year of cold sheet and strip. The last two investment projects provide another opportunity to install tinning lines with a capacity of 180 thousand metric tons per year at COSIPA and/or CSN.

Treatment of Investment Cost in the Model

Data on the cost of productive units used in the manufacture of flat steel products and a description of the use of these data for estimating the cost of the investment opportunities is given in Appendix E.

Once the cost of an investment project has been determined it is necessary to discount these costs to obtain the present value of cost of the project. Since the outlays for the project are normally made over a period of several years, while the project is being planned, equipment designed and constructed, buildings erected, and equipment installed and tested, the present value of cost calculations should be made by obtaining data on the stream of payments over time and discounting all of the payments to the present (January 1, 1965, in this model). However, as this sort of data is difficult to obtain, it is assumed that the payments are fairly evenly distributed about the midpoint of the "gestation period" for the project. As an approximation to this distribution, it will be assumed that all capital cost is concentrated at the midpoint of the gestation period, and this cost will then be discounted to January 1, 1965.[11]

For example, Table 6.8 lists as two years the gestation period for the project of installing a LD converter at COSIPA. That is, it was estimated that two years would be required to plan, construct, and install such a converter. Since the project would go into operation at the beginning of the second time period on July 1, 1967, it was assumed that the $7.9 million outlay for the project would all be made on July 1, 1966 (the midpoint of the two-year gestation period).

Since the model has a fixed horizon, a modification in the treatment of capital cost was necessary in order to avoid distorting edge effects. If the entire cost of investments made in the later time periods were charged in the planning period, the solutions would tend to favor imports or increased interplant shipments rather than investments. In order

[11] The present value at the midpoint is not the same as the present value of a cost stream that is evenly distributed about the midpoint but it is a sufficiently accurate approximation for our purposes.

to avoid these effects, capital costs have been converted to the equivalent uniform[12] payment series, and the payments have been cut off at the end of the period covered by the model. In effect, the system is only forced to pay for that portion of capital services that is utilized within the fixed time horizon of the model. Or, to express it another way, it is as though the system paid biannually for the use of the capital equipment during the life of the equipment. The discounted cost of the investment projects was calculated with the following functions. Let f_r be the arithmetic sum of the capital costs for the installation of the rth project, let R be the discount rate per six-month period,[13] let NZ be the expected life of the equipment in number of six-month periods, and let L be the size of the payments in the uniform series.[14] Then

$$L = f_r \frac{R(1 + R)^{NZ}}{(1 + R)^{NZ} - 1}.$$ (6.3)

Furthermore, let $D_r f_r$ be the present value of the cost of the project r, let M be the number of the six-month period (assuming January 1, 1965, to July 1, 1965, is the first six-month period — January 1, 1965, being the date to which all costs are discounted) which is the midpoint of the gestation period of the project, and let NQ be the number of six-month periods in the time spanned by the model. Then[15]

$$D_r f_r = \frac{L}{(1 + R)^M} + \frac{L}{(1 + R)^{M+1}} F \cdots + \frac{L}{(1 + R)^{\min (M+NZ, NQ)}}.$$ (6.4)

Take for example the investment project for a cold strip mill at CSN in the fourth time period. For this project $f_r = 10$, $NZ = 40$, and $NQ = 20$. The gestation time of the project is two years; thus, the time from the midpoint of the gestation period to completion of the project is two six-month periods. Since the project is to be completed by July 1, 1972 (the sixteenth six-month period of the twenty six-month periods between the date to which all costs are discounted and the end of the time span covered by the model), the investment can be treated as though all payments were made at the beginning of the fourteenth six-

[12] For cases in which the obsolescence rate is high, Alan Manne has suggested that a double declining balance would offer a better approximation than a *uniform* rental charge.

[13] If loans were available to purchase imported equipment, and such loans were not available for any other purpose, it would be appropriate to use different discount rates for different parts of the capital cost of the projects.

[14] Each time period of two and a half years was divided into five six-month periods.

[15] This method of discounting differs slightly from the preferred method that is discussed in Chapter 3.

month period.[16] Here R is assumed equal to 5 per cent (a discount rate of 10 per cent per year). Then

$$L = 10.0 \left[\frac{.05(1 + .05)^{40}}{(1 + .05)^{40} - 1} \right]$$

$$L = (10.0)(.0582)$$

$$L = .582$$

and

$$D_r f_r = .582 \left[\frac{1}{(1 + .05)^{13}} + \frac{1}{(1 + .05)^{14}} + \cdots + \frac{1}{(1 + .05)^{20}} \right]$$

$$D_r f_r = (.582)(3.598)$$

$$D_r f_r = \$2.095.$$

The Right-Hand-Side Capacities and Requirements

The vector of the right-hand side of the model consists of a series of elements specifying the capacities of the productive units and the requirements of the market areas in each time period. This is shown in Appendix F, Figure F.5. Also, the right-hand-side vector includes in its bottom section elements designed to constrain the integer variables to zero or one values. (See Figure F.6.)

The vectors of capacities are constant in all time periods unless it is anticipated that some productive units will be forced to shut down during the period covered by the model. A discussion of the meaning of the capacities is given at the beginning of Chapter 4.

The market requirements in each time period were based on projections for the consumption of rolled steel products. A number of studies

TABLE 6.9 Projections of Steel Consumption in Brazil for Rolled Steel Products
(*in millions of ingot metric tons*)

	1965	1970	1975
ILAFA	4.374	7.173	11.723
BISI	4.863	7.857	12.750
BNDE	4.382	6.841	10.630

have been made to forecast future consumption of steel products in Brazil. The results of three of these are shown in Table 6.9. The first

[16] A slight error was made in writing the computer program to perform these calculations with the result that all investments were treated as though they were made six months before the proper date. Therefore, the project is treated as though all payments were made at the beginning of the thirteenth six-month period and $M = 13$. The small magnitude of the resulting error was not deemed large enough to justify the cost of resolving the entire model with the correction.

was reported in a study mimeographed by ILAFA;[17] the second is an unpublished study done for the Brazilian Iron and Steel Institute;[18] and the third is an unpublished study done by Osao Komo of the Banco Nacional de Desenvolvimento (BNDE) of Brazil.[19]

The BNDE study was chosen as the basis for the market requirements used in this study. The basic equation of the BNDE projections is

$$\log y = 1.41393 \log x - 1.72297,$$

where y is the expected consumption of rolled steel products in millions of ingot metric tons and x is the amount of the gross national product that is generated in the construction and manufacturing industries.

The BNDE study assumes the following percentage breakdown of demand between flat products and shapes:

	1965	1970	1975
Shapes	53	51	50
Flats	47	49	50

This breakdown was applied to the projection given in Table 6.9 and separate calculations were made for tin plate to obtain the following projection for final products (in millions of *ingot* metric tons):

	1965	1970	1975
Plates, sheet, strip	1.709	2.805	4.465
Tin plate	.351	.547	.850

These data were converted to projections in millions of metric tons of *final* products by dividing the plates, sheets, and strips by 1.28 and the tin plate by 1.40. The results were then plotted on graph paper and smooth curves drawn between the points so as to obtain the values of the projections for mid-1967 and mid-1972. Table 6.10 gives the results.

Of the total amount of plates, sheets, and strips it was assumed that 25 per cent would be plate, 33 per cent would be hot sheet and strip, and 42 per cent would be cold sheet and strip. This percentage breakdown of the data in Table 6.10 yielded Table 6.11.

[17] Instituto Latinoamericano del Fierro y el Acero, "Estimación del consumo probable de acero laminado para los años 1965, 1970 y 1975," Santiago, Chile, 1964.

[18] Instituto Brasileiro de Siderurgia, Viaduto Dona Paulina 80, São Paulo, Brazil, 1964.

[19] Banco Nacional de Desenvolvimento, Economic Department, Rua Sete de Setembre, 48 Rio de Janeiro, Brazil.

TABLE 6.10 PROJECTIONS OF CONSUMPTION OF FLAT STEEL PRODUCTS IN BRAZIL (*millions of tons of final products*)

	1965	Mid-1967	1970	Mid-1972	1975
Plates, sheet, strip	1.332	1.750	2.190	2.770	3.490
Tin plate	.250	.310	.391	.490	.607
Total	1.582	2.060	2.581	3.260	4.097

Two further assumptions were needed to complete the calculation of the market requirements. The first of these was that 100 per cent of the consumption of flat products in Brazil occurs in the "southern triangle" of Brazil bounded by São Paulo, Rio de Janeiro, and Belo Horizonte.

TABLE 6.11 PROJECTIONS OF BRAZILIAN CONSUMPTION OF FLAT STEEL PRODUCTS (*millions of tons of final products*)

	1965	Mid-1967	1970	Mid-1972	1975
Plates	.332	.437	.547	.693	.872
Hot sheet and strip	.440	.579	.722	.914	1.150
Cold sheet and strip	.560	.734	.920	1.162	1.468
Tin plate	.250	.310	.392	.490	.607
Total	1.582	2.060	2.581	3.260	4.097

This assumption doubtlessly overstated the concentration of flat-product-using industries in Brazil, but only slightly. Second, it was necessary to make assumptions about the distribution of consumption for flat steel products among the three market areas that comprise the "southern triangle." These are shown in Table 6.12 and are based on some guesses about the distribution that were made by Brazilian steel men and sug-

TABLE 6.12 REGIONAL BREAKDOWN OF CONSUMPTION OF FLAT STEEL PRODUCTS
(*percentage of total consumption in the southern triangle*)

	São Paulo	Rio de Janeiro	Belo Horizonte
Plate	30	50	20
Hot sheet and strip	60	25	15
Cold sheet and strip	65	20	15
Tin plate	70	20	10

gested to the author. The application of these assumptions to the results already given yielded the market requirements used in the model. Table 6.13 shows these requirements.

TABLE 6.13 PROJECTIONS OF PRODUCT REQUIREMENTS FOR FLAT STEEL PRODUCTS (*millions of tons of final products*)

Market and Product	1965	Mid-1967	1970	Mid-1972	1975
São Paulo					
Plate	.100	.131	.164	.208	.262
Hot	.264	.347	.433	.548	.690
Cold	.364	.476	.598	.756	.954
Tin	.175	.217	.274	.343	.425
Rio de Janeiro					
Plate	.166	.218	.274	.347	.436
Hot	.110	.145	.181	.228	.288
Cold	.112	.147	.184	.233	.294
Tin	.050	.062	.078	.098	.121
Belo Horizonte					
Plate	.066	.087	.109	.139	.174
Hot	.066	.087	.108	.137	.172
Cold	.084	.111	.138	.174	.220
Tin	.025	.031	.039	.049	.061

7

Solutions to the Multiperiod Model

Two versions of the model were set up for solution. One version had eleven integer variables, the other twenty-three; otherwise the two versions were identical. The first version used the investment opportunities available in periods 2 and 3 and assumed that no investment opportunities existed in the fourth time period; the second version used those available in periods 2, 3, and 4.

The models were first solved as a regular linear programming problem to obtain linear solutions with upper bounds of unity on the investment variables. This was done because there was reason to believe that problems which appear to be difficult integer programming problems often have continuous solutions (that is, solutions in which the integer constraints are not activated) so close to a lattice point[1] that it is not necessary to employ integer programming algorithms to solve them.

Second, attempts were made to solve the problems with Driebeek's mixed-integer programming algorithm.[2] Then with the heuristic mixed-integer solution from the algorithm in hand, some additional lattice point solutions to the problem were obtained through the use of the computer time-sharing system of Project MAC.

---

[1] We use lattice point here to refer to a point in the solution space at which the investment decision variables take on integer values and all other variables are free to take on any nonnegative values.

[2] The author is indebted to N. Driebeek for permission to use his algorithm. A description of this algorithm is given in Norman J. Driebeek, "An Algorithm for the Solution of Mixed Integer Programming Problems," *Management Science*, Vol. 12, No. 7 (March 1966), pp. 576–687.

Driebeek's Algorithm

Driebeek's algorithm is a search routine for finding that lattice point which is the global optimum of the problem. It begins by calculating a continuous solution to the problem with the integer variables constrained to take on values less than or equal to one (and greater than or equal to zero — by the nonnegativity constraint). From this solution a set of penalties is calculated. For a cost-minimizing problem these penalties represent lower bounds on the additional cost (over and above the value of the objective function for the continuous solution) to the system that forces the investment variables to take on integer values.

Two classes of penalties are calculated: "true" and "pseudo" penalties. The "true" penalties are associated with those investment variables that are at the upper or lower bound in the continuous solution. For those variables in the continuous solution at the upper bound, the shadow price on the row that constrains the variable to be less than or equal to one represents the minimum amount that the functional value would have to increase if the variable were forced from one to zero. The change in the functional value will be greater than the magnitude of the associated shadow price if the act of forcing the variable to zero results in some basic change of the continuous variables.

For investment variables at the zero level in the continuous solution, the "true" penalty for leaving it at zero is itself zero, and the penalty for forcing it to one is at least as great as the value of the "reduced cost" for the variable. The "reduced cost" is a lower bound on the change in the value of the objective function that would result from forcing a variable at the zero level into the solution at a level of unity.[3]

The "pseudo" penalties, which are associated with the variables that are in the continuous solution at fractional values, are calculated with the equation

$$(\bar{\alpha}_{ij} - 1.0)\cdot \max_k \left(\frac{d_k}{a_{rk}}\right) \qquad k = 1, 2, \cdots, n; (k|a_{rk} < 0), \qquad (7.1)$$

"where $A = [a_{jk}]$ is the updated matrix at the continuous optimum, d_k is the reduced cost of the kth variable at the continuous optimum solution, and r is the index of the row currently occupied by α_{ij} in the

---

[3] Weingartner has pointed out that the shadow prices on rows used to constrain the investment variables to be less than or equal to one and "reduced cost" on the investment variables might be useful for ranking projects. Though the "reduced cost" does not by itself provide a reliable ranking for projects, it can be used to great advantage in providing bounds on the solution. See his *Mathematical Programming and the Analysis of Capital Budgeting Problems* (Englewood Cliffs, N.J.: Prentice-Hall, Inc., 1963), p. 55.

basis."[4] In Driebeek's notation the variable α_{ij} is the slack variable associated with the jth dormant integer constraint row for the ith integer variable. If the integer variable is permitted to take on integer values up to n, there are $n + 1$ dormant integer rows. Here $\bar{\alpha}_{ij}$ is the value of the variable in the continuous solution.

Once the penalty table is constructed, it is used to select an "original" combination of investments. The integer level that corresponds to the penalty with the smallest absolute value is selected for each integer variable. The integer constraint rows are utilized to force the integer variables to the chosen values, and the problem is solved. The value of the objective function for this integer solution and the functional value for the continuous solution then provide upper and lower bounds for the value of the objective function with the "best" integer solution. In a minimizing problem the continuous solution gives the lower bound and the initial integer solution gives the upper bound.

The difference between the value of the objective function for the continuous solution and the functional value for the integer solution is then compared to the penalties. If any variable has a penalty greater than the difference between the values of the functional for the continuous and the best known integer solutions, then that variable must be at its present integer level in the optimum solution. This device enables the Driebeek algorithm to reduce drastically (in some problems) the number of lattice points that must be investigated.

Once a continuous and an original integer solution are obtained, then a complete enumeration of all unbounded lattice points is undertaken. Each time another lattice point is selected it is checked to see if it is bounded out. If it is not, then dual iterations are performed to restore feasibility. If the value of the objective function goes above the value of the function obtained with the best previous integer solution, the trial is cut off and another lattice point is selected. The algorithm proceeds in this fashion until all of the eligible lattice points have been tested or until the run is halted.

Computational Experience with Driebeek's Algorithm

The eleven-integer-variable version of the problem was attempted first. A continuous and a first mixed-integer solution were found, and the difference between the functional values for these two solutions was small enough and some of the penalties were large enough to permit the bounding out of four of the eleven integer variables. Thus, the number of lattice points to be inspected was reduced from 2,048 to 128. About 100 of the remaining 128 points were tested, a process requiring

[4] Driebeek, *op. cit.*, p. 580.

slightly less than one hour on an IBM 7094. In addition to the 11 integer variables, the problem contained 122 constraints, 433 other variables, and slightly fewer than 1,800 matrix entries.

In the second version of the model the number of integer variables was increased to 23. After trying 33 lattice points, a solution was found that had a functional value close enough to the functional value on the continuous solution of the problem to bound off 7,863,720 of the 8,388,608 lattice points. An additional 22 lattice points were inspected before the run was halted. Therefore, while the solution obtained is good, it may or may not be the best one. To prove that it is the best solution one would have to inspect all or part of the remaining 524,833 lattice points.

The Use of Time Sharing[5]

When a search routine is used to solve a problem and when the problem is too large to make an exhaustive search, one feels uncertain about the result, no matter how impressive the performance of the algorithm has been on similar problems with known solutions. Also, with this type of mixed-integer problem in which there is a relatively small number of integer variables, the model builder often has an intuitive feel for those combinations of integers that are most likely to form the optimum combination. When this intuition is aided by an algorithm to guide the model builder to a lattice point (which, if it is not the optimum is very close to it) the result may be much better than if only the algorithm were used or if only intuition were used.

The capabilities of a time-sharing system lend themselves very well to this kind of algorithm-intuition approach. Driebeek's algorithm produces upper and lower bounds on the solution, and intuition may be used to narrow the difference between these bounds. For this reason, with the results from the use of the algorithm in hand, a program was written to permit the console operator on the time-sharing system to modify the right-hand side of the problem so as to force the solution to a chosen lattice point.[6] This program and the linear programming routine RSMFOR, with which it is used, have the capablity of using multiple right-hand sides, that is, of solving a linear programming problem, altering some or all of the elements in the right-hand side, and running

---

[5] A time-sharing system is a computer system in which many remote consoles are attached to a central computer. Each user receives what appears to him to be almost continuous service from the central computer.

[6] This program as well as the input-smoothing and output-smoothing programs prepared for the mixed-integer programming model were written by David Kelleher, to whom the author is indebted for excellent programming work.

the program again. With this model the linear programming routine required about 90 seconds with an IBM 7094 to reach the first optimal solution but only 10–20 seconds to obtain each additional optimal solution. Thus the model builder can use the results of the algorithm solution and try in rapid succession a number of lattice points that he feels offer a better solution than that obtained by the algorithm.

An economic planning office, be it in a private firm or in a national government, is often faced with the task of presenting alternatives and the associated cost of each alternative. The time-sharing system offers the capability of obtaining results from a number of combinations with the opportunity of looking at the results almost immediately, and of choosing on the basis of those results other combinations of investments that might be interesting to examine.

Often those charged with the decisions on investment alternatives wish to consider many noneconomic criteria in their decisions. When those criteria are such that they cannot be programmed into the problem, the time-sharing system may offer a very useful tool. It is simple enough to operate, so that with well-designed response programs[7] a decision maker who is otherwise unfamiliar with computation can be instructed easily in the use of the system. He may not be as interested in obtaining a single optimum solution as in knowing the relative resource cost of different alternatives. In such cases it may be useful to formulate very large mixed-integer programming problems without intending to find a global optimum with certainty but rather to use the problem as a simulation device.

A Solution to the Problem

Since computation cost prohibited the enumeration of all of the unbounded lattice points to the problem with twenty-three variables, we do not know whether the mixed-integer solution we obtained is the optimum solution. However, we have two pieces of evidence which indicate that the mixed-integer solution we have found is a good one, that is, close to the optimum:

1. The algorithm has performed well in solving smaller problems with a known solution.

2. Since the difference between the functional value for the continuous solution to the problem ($759.45 million) and the functional value for our mixed-integer solution ($769.37 million) is about $10 million, costs cannot be reduced by more than this amount.

[7] Response programs are programs that respond to inquiries of the operator and carry out actions indicated by him.

TABLE 7.1   ACTIVITY LEVELS FOR DECISION VARIABLES

Decision Variables	Second Period July 1967–Jan. 1970		Third Period Jan. 1970–July 1972		Fourth Period July 1972–Jan. 1975	
Blast furnace modifications			COSIPA	Yes		
			USIMINAS	Yes		
New blast furnace					COSIPA	Yes
					USIMINAS	Yes
					CSN	No
First and second oxygen converter			CSN	No	CSN	No
Third oxygen converter	COSIPA	No	COSIPA	Yes		
	USIMINAS	Yes	USIMINAS	Yes		
Fourth and fifth oxygen converter					COSIPA	No
					USIMINAS	No
Added stand for roughing mill					COSIPA	Yes
Cold strip mill					COSIPA	Yes
					USIMINAS	Yes
					CSN	No
Tinning line	COSIPA	Yes	COSIPA	No	COSIPA	No
	CSN	No	CSN	Yes	CSN	No

With this in mind we turn our attention to the best known mixed-integer solution to this problem with twenty-three investment variables. Table 7.1 gives the activity levels for the decision variables.

Of the five projects for increases in capacity in blast furnaces, either through modification of existing furnaces or through installation of new furnaces, four were chosen for execution. Only the construction of a new blast furnace at the CSN plant at Volta Redonda, scheduled to go into operation at the beginning of the fourth time period (July 1972), was rejected.

Since added capacity in the steel shops could be obtained for less cost through the addition of a third oxygen converter in plants with an existing pair rather than through the installation of a pair of converters at CSN, these projects were chosen.[8]

The tinning line section at the bottom of Table 7.1 shows that the projects for installation of a tinning line at COSIPA in 1967 and at CSN in 1970 were approved. This distribution of investments over time and space takes advantage of the interdependencies between projects and is the type of solution that one expects.

Six of the ten projects for COSIPA and five of the six projects for

---

[8] Failure to constrain the model to prevent the installation of a third oxygen converter in subsequent periods at a single plant resulted in projects being accepted for a third oxygen converter at USIMINAS in both the second and third time periods. Such a constraint should be added in any additional runs of the model.

USIMINAS were approved, while only one of the seven projects for CSN was accepted. Projects for investments in the blast furnaces and steel shop at Brazil's oldest integrated steel mill at CSN were systematically rejected in favor of additions to capacity in these primary units at the two newer plants of COSIPA and USIMINAS. There are at least three possible explanations for this result, two of which are fairly obvious and a third that is not so obvious.

The most obvious explanation is that *under the assumptions of the model* the cost of production for steel products is greater at CSN than at either COSIPA or at USIMINAS. The difference is so large that, even with the proximity of CSN to the large market area of Rio de Janeiro, USIMINAS can produce and deliver steel products to Rio at a lower cost than CSN. Thus, perhaps it was desirable to install new capacity at the plants which, over the long run, would be able to supply the market areas at less cost to the country.

Second, the investment projects in the primary units at CSN may have been rejected in favor of those at COSIPA and USIMINAS because of the structure of capacity in the three plants. As the oldest plant of the three, CSN was using almost all of the capacity in its primary productive units to the fullest extent. Thus, if more capacity were installed in the steel shop, additional capacity would at the same time have to be installed in pig iron production and in a new primary mill. The plants of COSIPA and USIMINAS, on the other hand, had excess capacity in a number of units and the capability of making relatively inexpensive modifications to existing primary units to add substantially to their capacity. Thus, increments to national capacity could be made at the least cost to the country in the short run through additions to capacity in these plants.

The phrase "in the short run" in the previous paragraph is the key to the third and less obvious explanation for the solution. The objective was to minimize the total production and transportation cost of meeting the steel requirements of the country during the period covered by the model. Therefore, the cost of meeting the steel needs of Brazil in the years after 1975 did not enter the calculations. Thus, if the needs of the system could be met in the short run by expanding the existing plants piecemeal rather than by constructing the basis for even greater expansions in the distant future, this would be the strategy that would be followed. For this reason, there is much to be said for building a model to cover a period of time somewhat longer than the period for which investment decisions must be made.[9]

[9] Alternatively, one might build into the model terminal corrections of the sort suggested in a Ph.D. thesis currently in preparation by Henry Jacoby of Harvard University on the analysis of interdependent investments in the electric power industry.

TABLE 7.2 ACTIVITY LEVELS FOR PRODUCTION: TRANSPORTATION ACTIVITIES
(*millions of metric tons per year*)

Activity	Second Time Period	Third Time Period	Fourth Time Period
Group 1			
COSIPA, CSN, Pig iron	.002		
COSIPA, CSN, Slabs		.083	
USIMINAS, COSIPA, Ingot steel			.200
USIMINAS, COSIPA, Slabs			.335
USIMINAS, CSN, Pig iron	.061		
USIMINAS, CSN, Slabs		.097	.178
CSN, COSIPA, Ingot steel	.220	.135	
Group 2			
Imports, COSIPA, Slabs	.017		
Group 3			
COSIPA, São Paulo, Plate	.131	.125	.208
COSIPA, São Paulo, Hot sheet	.347	.433	.548
COSIPA, São Paulo, Cold sheet		.278	.511
COSIPA, São Paulo, Tin plate	.167	.058	.157
COSIPA, Rio de Janeiro, Plate			.157
Group 4			
USIMINAS, Rio de Janeiro, Plate	.074		
USIMINAS, Rio de Janeiro, Hot sheet	.145	.166	.090
USIMINAS, Rio de Janeiro, Cold sheet		.008	.061
USIMINAS, Belo Horizonte, Plate	.087	.109	.139
USIMINAS, Belo Horizonte, Hot sheet	.087	.108	.137
USIMINAS, Belo Horizonte, Cold sheet	.111	.138	.174
Group 5			
CSN, São Paulo, Plate		.039	
CSN, São Paulo, Cold sheet	.476	.320	.245
CSN, São Paulo, Tin plate	.050	.216	.186
CSN, Rio de Janeiro, Plate	.144	.274	.190
CSN, Rio de Janeiro, Hot sheet		.014	.138
CSN, Rio de Janeiro, Cold sheet	.147	.097	.172
CSN, Rio de Janeiro, Tin plate	.062	.078	.098
CSN, Belo Horizonte, Tin plate	.031	.039	.049
Group 6			
Imports, Rio de Janeiro, Cold sheet		.079	
Group 7			
COSIPA, Exports, Hot sheet			.157
COSIPA, Exports, Pig iron			.364
COSIPA, Exports, Cold sheet	.159		
USIMINAS, Exports, Pig iron			.200
USIMINAS, Exports, Slabs		.071	
USIMINAS, Exports, Hot sheet	.176	.379	.038
USIMINAS, Exports, Cold sheet	.034		.251

Table 7.2 gives the activity levels for the production-transportation activities in the three time periods. The capability of shipping intermediate products between plants was much used. The products being shipped and the sending and receiving plants changed from one time period to another as new production units were installed, thereby shifting the capacity bottleneck in the plant from one productive unit to another.

The Group 3 activities in the table show that in the second and third time periods COSIPA would provide final products only to the nearby market of São Paulo but in the fourth period would begin to provide some steel plate to the Rio de Janeiro market. CSN at Volta Redonda, on the other hand, is shown to have a decreasing share of the São Paulo market area (Group 5).

The changes in flow of products from plants to market areas across different time periods reflect the degree of interdependence of the investments in the system and show how the operation of the system might change under a given pattern of investments. An example of this type of phenomenon was discussed in the test on the single-period model in Chapter 5.

The activity levels for exports (Group 7) approximate expected developments for the decade to come. For example, all of the exporting is done by COSIPA and USIMINAS, the two plants that are in the best locations for exporting. It does not appear that under the present assumptions of the model there is sufficient incentive for Brazil to build up a large export industry in steel products. If a number of the investment opportunities available had not been rejected, the failure to build up capacity for exporting would be less convincing. A study of the effects on the model of increases and/or decreases in the profitability of exporting should prove to be interesting.

Improvements in the Model

This work points the way to a number of improvements that could be made in this type of investment planning model. The assumption of a price elasticity of demand of zero needs to be relaxed. A quadratic programming approach could be useful; but this raises the problem of how one might combine quadratic and mixed-integer programming. Also, the assumptions that the supply of imports and the demand for exports are perfectly elastic need to be modified. More feedback is needed from the choice of investments to the cost of production. In the present model this operates only through decisions to make investments at one plant rather than at another. The feedback should also operate from the choice of investment within a plant to the cost of the production activities. This modification could be made either through the use of some additional integer variables in the model or through the iteration of the solutions to the model. Also, it could be most useful to incorporate some of the recent progress in methods of stochastic programming into this type of decision model. Finally, though the computational problems would be increased substantially, the assumption of linear cost function could be modified through the use of piecewise linear functions provided the costs were increasing functions of the activity levels.[10]

Conclusions

For many years economists have been of the opinion that indivisibilities and economies of scale should be incorporated into investment planning models but they have not been able to achieve this in an effective manner because of the computational difficulties involved. This study has demonstrated that it is possible to construct tight upper and lower bounds on solutions to multiperiod, multiproduct sectoral models for studying discrete additions to capacity through investments in existing plants and/or the addition of new plants to the system. And for problems where the number of integer variables can be limited to a sufficiently small number, it has been shown that an optimal solution may be obtained. The flexibility of these mixed-integer programming models makes them useful tools for studying questions of investment under economies of scale, discrete investment, import substitution, installation of domestic capacity for exporting intermediate and final products, and choice of technology.

We have also shown that the advent of time-sharing systems for large computers adds another valuable tool to the available methods for studying investment problems. The use of a bounding algorithm together with intuition is shown to be a very useful device in obtaining good solutions to mixed-integer programming problems. Also, time-sharing systems are shown to provide the possibility of obtaining cost estimates on a great variety of investment strategies within a few minutes. Thus, it becomes easy for an analyst to make the calculations for a wide variety of choices that can then be submitted to the policy makers (be they corporate managers or politicians) for decision.

[10] See Weingartner, *op. cit.*, pp. 134–138.

APPENDIXES

Appendix A

A Brief Description of the Production of Flat Steel Products

As our purpose here is to provide only the necessary glossary for an understanding of the terms used in this book, the reader who is interested in making a detailed study of steel technology is referred to a publication of the United States Steel Corporation, *The Making, Shaping, and Treating of Steel* (originally written by Camp and Francis).

The production of steel products may be divided into four basic processes: (1) the mining and preparation of raw materials, (2) the reduction of iron ore to pig iron, (3) the refining of pig iron to steel, and (4) the rolling of the steel ingots to shape them into final products.

The Mining and Preparation of Raw Materials

Iron ore is mined in open-pit mines and is usually crushed and sized near the mines. The ores are transported to the steel mill where the lump ores may be charged directly to the blast furnace and the ore fines (fine particles of ore) are mixed with coal fines and agglomerated to produce a high-quality and uniformly sized input for the blast furnace. This mixture of ore fines and coal fines, called *sinter,* is widely used in Latin America. Also, a few pelletizing plants are being constructed to concentrate the ores into uniformly sized pellets. Pelletizing has not been adopted rapidly in the region because Latin American ores are generally of such high iron content that pelletizing has not been deemed economic.

In many countries in the region national coals contain such a high percentage of volatile material that it is necessary to mix them with imported coals in order to have a cokable mixture. The coals are mixed before they are heated in coke ovens to produce *coke* and *coke gas.* A number of chemical by-products are extracted from the coke gas and the remaining gas is used for heating purposes elsewhere in the plant.

101

The Reduction of Iron Ore to Pig Iron

Coke, iron ore (and/or sinter and/or pellets), and limestone constitute the principal materials charged to the *reduction furnace,* which is usually a *blast furnace,* though at least two major plants in Latin America have *electric reduction furnaces.*

The ore and coke is charged at the top of the blast furnace and a blast of heated air is forced in through openings in the sides of the furnace near the bottom and forced up through the charge. Often petroleum or natural gas is injected through these openings along with the blast. The ores are reduced (that is, oxygen is removed from the iron oxide ores to reduce them to purer forms of iron) in the furnace and molten *pig iron* is tapped from the bottom of the furnace. Also, molten *slag* is tapped from the bottom of the furnace and may be sold for use in cement manufacturing or for other industrial purposes.

The blast is converted to *blast furnace gas,* a gas of a relatively low specific heat, as it is forced up through the furnace. The gas leaves the furnace at the top, is cleaned, and is then passed through a series of heat exchangers that are used to heat the incoming blast. Only about one-third of the blast furnace gas is required to heat the incoming blast. Therefore, the remainder is used elsewhere in the plant or sold to other plants for use as a fuel.

The Refining of Pig Iron to Steel

The molten pig iron is transported in special railroad cars to the steel furnaces (sometimes called the steel shop). There it is poured into huge ladles and transported to the furnaces. The majority of the integrated steel plants in Latin America have *open-hearth steel furnaces.* These furnaces are shaped like great baths. They are charged with molten pig iron, scrap, ferroalloys, iron ore, and limestone. Then hot air or flames are blown across the bath to maintain it at very high temperatures. Oil is often used as a fuel, though a mixture of coke and/or blast furnace gases or other types of fuels may be used.

The average time for a *heat,* that is, the time from one charge to the next, averages from eight to eleven hours. Many plants have reduced this time by a matter of hours by injecting oxygen through lances in the roof of the furnace.

There is a marked tendency for new plants to install *LD* (Linz-Donawitz) *converters* rather than open-hearth furnaces. An LD converter is something like the more familiar *Bessemer converter* except that oxygen rather than air is injected into the furnace and the injection is through a lance from the top rather than through openings in the bottom of the converter. The LD converters, because of their very short heat time, have a substantially smaller capital cost per unit of output than the open hearths. The open hearths, on the other hand, are said to be able to operate with higher percentages of scrap content in the charge.

A few steel mills in the region use *electric steel furnaces*. These furnaces are charged from the top with molten pig iron, scrap, and so on. Carbon *electrodes* protrude through the roof of the furnace down into the charge, and electric current is arced between these electrodes to heat the charge.

The hot metal is discharged from the steel furnace into a ladle, and the ladle is transported by an overhead crane to an area where its contents are poured into *ingot molds*. The molten metal is allowed to cool sufficiently so that when the mold is stripped off it leaves a solid *ingot* of steel. The ingot is usually of rectangular cross section and about eight to ten feet high.

The Shaping of the Steel Ingots to Make Final Products

Within the last few years some steel plants in Latin America have installed *continuous casting plants*. In these plants the molten metal is poured from the ladle into a container that feeds a continuous flow of liquid steel into a vertical column. The steel hardens as it descends and is cut off at the bottom of the mold. Though first used only for light shapes, this method is now being adopted for the production of large slabs as well.

In the more conventional mills the ingots are transported to *soaking pits* where they are heated until they attain uniform temperatures throughout. The ingot is removed from the soaking pit by overhead cranes and taken to the *primary mill,* where it is flattened and elongated by being rolled back and forth through the mill as the rollers are brought closer together on each pass. The process forms the ingot into either *blooms* or *slabs*. Blooms are square in cross section and are used for producing *shapes* (angles, rods, beams, pipe, rails), while slabs are rectangular in cross section and are used for producing *flat products* (sheets, strip, plate, coils, tin plate). A primary mill that is used principally for producing blooms is called a *blooming mill,* and a mill used for shaping slabs is called a *slabbing mill.*

Since a continuous casting unit replaces the ingot molds, soaking pits, and primary mill, it offers large savings in capital cost over conventional methods. Also, because of reduced scrap losses, it reduces operating cost.

The slabs produced either by the conventional method or by continuous casting are allowed to cool, and then are cleaned, checked, and stacked in the slab yard to await further rolling. There are several reasons for permitting the product to cool at this point. First, it is important to check the slabs carefully for flaws that may have resulted from faults in the ingots. Second, the outside edges of the slabs may leave slight marks on the rollers, so it is desirable, when possible, to schedule the rolling in such a fashion as to roll from wide to narrow, that is, to roll the widest products first and then move down to the narrower products.

Once the slab is selected for rolling it is shoved into a *reheating furnace* where it remains until it is heated uniformly. It is then passed through a small mill called a *scale breaker* before entering the *roughing mill* (or *plate mill*). The mill may be either reversible, semicontinuous, or continuous. A *reversible rougher* passes the product back and forth through the mill rolling it thinner with each pass. This mill may be either a *two-high* or a *three-high*. The two-high mill has two rollers, which are reversed each time the product is reversed. The three-high mill does not require a reversing of the three rollers. Instead, the tables on each side of the mill lower or raise the product to feed it through the mill first in one direction then in the other.

A *semicontinuous roughing mill* usually consists of a reversing rougher followed by a single-pass mill. In some of the newer mills either a reversing or a semicontinuous rougher has been installed with space provided for the addition of more mills to the line. Thus, a semicontinuous mill may be converted easily to a *continuous mill,* in which the product moves continuously through a number of mills (or *stands*). As a rough estimate one might say that a plant with a capacity of less than half a million metric tons per year would be equipped with a reversing rougher, a one-million-ton plant would be equipped with a semicontinuous rougher, and plants with more than one and a half million tons of capacity would have a continuous rougher.

The part of the product that is to be sold as *plate* leaves the main line at this point and is passed through a plate mill, where very little reduction in thickness takes place but where the product is smoothed before being cut, checked, and prepared for shipment.

The part of the product that continues down the main line from the roughing mill passes to the *finishing mill,* which may be either reversible or continuous. A reversible finishing mill is often called a *Steckle mill* after its inventor. A Steckle mill is a *four-high* mill (two smaller *working rolls,* through which the product passes, backed up by two larger rollers) with a *coiler* on each side of the mill. The product is passed back and forth through the mill until it is reduced enough to be rolled up on one of the coilers. Then it is reversed, being unrolled from the one coiler, reduced as it passes through the mill, and then rolled up on the coiler on the other side. Because of their relative slowness Steckle mills are used ordinarily in plants with a capacity of less than half a million tons per year.

A *continuous finishing mill* (sometimes called a *hot strip mill*) consists of four, five, or six stands placed about twenty feet apart. Each of these stands is a four-high mill. The product shoots through these stands at a speed of about twenty-five miles per hour, being slightly reduced in thickness at each stand. The product leaving the mill is called *hot sheet* or *hot strip*. After leaving the hot strip mill it is either cut and packaged or it is rolled up into coils. The sheet may be as much as six feet or more in width, though four feet is a more common width. The largest users of this product are automobile and appliance factories.

The product that is destined for further processing is transported in coils to the *pickling line,* a sulphuric acid solution bath that cleans and deoxidizes the product. Most pickling lines are continuous; that is, the end of one coil is welded to the beginning of the next. Then at the other end of the bath the product is cut again and rerolled in coils.

The coils then advance to the *cold reduction mill* (often called a *cold strip mill*). Cold reduction mills normally consist of three to five stands (each stand being a four-high mill) placed about six feet apart. As with the continuous hot strip mill, the product is reduced slightly in thickness as it passes through each mill.

Since in the cold reduction mill the product is rolled at room temperature, it is hardened and becomes somewhat brittle. Therefore, the coils are taken from the cold reduction mill to the group of *annealing furnaces,* where they are soaked in heat for a number of hours to provide the desired degree of ductility. The coils are removed and are given a finishing pass in a *temper mill* — a single-stand mill. The cold sheets and strip may then be sold as coils; they may be cut and packaged for sale or they may be sent on to the *tinning line* or to the *galvanizing line.*

The galvanizing line prepares the product to be sold as galvanized sheets, mostly for construction purposes. The tinning line may be either batch or continuous. If it is a batch line, the product is cut into small sheets before it is dipped in molten tin to be coated. The continuous lines are referred to as *electrolytic tinning lines* as the tin plating is accomplished by an electrolytic process. Since a large percentage of tin products are used for making food containers, very careful inspection of the tin plate for pinholes or other defects is necessary. Electronic devices to do this checking have not yet been perfected; therefore, it must be done by hand, thereby increasing sharply the labor intensiveness of tin products.

Appendix B

Specific Inputs and Unit Cost of Inputs

Part I. Raw Data for Specific Inputs and Unit Cost of Inputs

Specific Inputs

Blast Furnaces. Table B.1 gives the raw data for specific inputs. The information for COSIPA was supplied by the firm and is theoretical, as the blast furnace at the plant was not yet in operation in February of

TABLE B.1 SPECIFIC INPUTS: BLAST FURNACES
(units of input per metric ton of pig iron)

Input (in metric tons except where noted)	COSIPA	USIMINAS with 70% Sinter	USIMINAS with 100% Sinter	CSN	CSN	CSN
Regular iron ore	.700	.470	—	40%	.782	—
Sinter	.760	1.100	1.500	60%	.794	.692
National coal	—	—	—	40%	.513	—
Imported coal	—	—	—	60%	.655	—
Coke	.680	.600	.560	.631	.764	.787
Dolomite	—	—	—	—	.035	—
Limestone	.400	.132	.100	—	.272	—
Manganese	.025	.040	.030	—	.018	—
Fuel oil (liters)	—	—	—	16.6	—	—
Electrical energy (1000 kwh)	.007	—	.070	—	—	—
Water (1000 m³)*	.650	—	.100	—	—	—
Steam	.020	—	.003	—	—	—
Blast furnace gas (1000 m³)	−3.300	—	—	—	−3.715	—
Slag	−0.430	—	—	—	−0.476	—
Blast temperature (°C)	980	800	—	800	—	—

* One thousand cubic meters.

1965 when the data were received. This vector of specific inputs does not include fuel oil injection since this equipment was not originally installed in the blast furnace.

There may be an error in the estimate of the specific consumption of water. The estimate was 650 cubic meters per ton of pig iron as compared to the normal estimate of 100 cubic meters or less. Therefore it appears that this is a decimal point error in the estimates and that the figure should be 65 cubic meters per ton of pig iron. The estimate of electrical energy consumption may also be off by a factor of 10; however, this is less certain. The estimate for COSIPA is 7 kilowatt hours per ton of pig iron. A comparison of this to an estimate of 70 kilowatt hours per ton of pig iron for the new USIMINAS blast furnace and an estimate of 35 kilowatt hours per ton of pig iron made in an unpublished Mexican study leads one to believe that this statistic may be off by a decimal point.

The data for USIMINAS were collected by the author while visiting the plant near Ipatinga in January of 1965. Two vectors of specific inputs are shown, one for a 70 per cent sinter charge and one for a 100 per cent sinter charge. The blast furnace had been operated with sinter charges of both percentages, so these data reflected the actual operating experience of the plant. Neither of these input vectors includes petroleum injection. Engineers in the plant estimated that the coke rate could be lowered to less than 500 kilograms per ton of pig iron once fuel oil injection was used.

The three columns of inputs shown for the blast furnaces of CSN at Volta Redonda are for observations from three different sources. The left-hand column gives information collected by the author while visiting the plant in January of 1965. However, this information is not of the same technical quality as that obtained at the USIMINAS plant. Higher quality information is shown in the middle column. These data were calculated from a flow sheet showing total input and output flows at the Volta Redonda plant in 1962. Since that date fuel oil injection has been installed in the blast furnaces at this plant, so there have probably been significant changes in the specific consumption of a number of the inputs. The data in the third column were taken from an article published in the May 1964 issue of *Revista* of the Latin American Iron and Steel Institute (p. 22).

Steel Furnaces. Table B.2 gives the specific inputs for the production of steel in the LD furnaces of COSIPA and USIMINAS and in the open-hearth furnaces of CSN at Volta Redonda.

The data for COSIPA in the first column of the table are theoretical because the LD furnaces of the plant were not yet in operation at the time the company prepared the data in January of 1965. They compare

TABLE B.2   SPECIFIC INPUTS: STEEL FURNACES
(units of input per metric ton of ingot steel)

Input (in metric tons except where noted)	COSIPA LD Furnace	USIMINAS LD Furnace	USIMINAS LD Furnace	CSN Open-Hearth Furnace	CSN Open-Hearth Furnace
Regular iron ore	.04	.020	.005	.106	.111
Regular scrap	.22	.169	.187	.358	.276
Return scrap	—	.015	.014	—	.030
Pig iron — liquid	.88	.959	.929	.698	.628
Pig iron — ingots	.016	—	—	—	.097
Dolomite	—	—	.006	—	—
Limestone	.08	—	.001	.042	.042
Quicklime	.08	.054	.059	—	—
Aluminum	.045	—	—	—	—
Fluorspar	.008	—	.004	—	—
Ferromanganese	.007	—	—	—	—
Ferrosilicon	.0006	—	—	—	—
Oxygen (1000 m³)*	.057	.055	.050	—	—
Electrical energy (1000 kwh)	.022	.019	.017	—	—
Water (1000 m³)	.016	—	.029	—	—
Steel shop refractories	.008	—	.007	.035	.043
Coke gas (1000 m³)	—	—	.020	—	—
Direct labor (man-hours)	—	—	1.98	—	—

* One thousand cubic meters.

closely, however, with the operating experience of the LD furnaces at USIMINAS.

Two vectors of inputs are shown for USIMINAS. The left-hand column of data was given to the author by officials at the company headquarters in Belo Horizonte. The right-hand column of information was obtained at the plant near Ipatinga in January of 1965. It is supposed that the data supplied by the company headquarters represent the experience of an earlier period in the performance of the furnaces.

The left-hand column of observations for CSN are from data collected by the author at the Volta Redonda plant in January of 1965. The right-hand column of figures were calculated from the flow sheet for the plant for 1962. The data calculated from the flow sheet provide a more detailed breakdown of the metallic charge to the open-hearth furnaces than do the data collected at the plant. Neither vector shows oxygen injection to the open-hearth furnaces. In January of 1965 three of the eight open-hearth furnaces were equipped with oxygen injection equipment. The oxygen plant had sufficient capacity to provide injection to only one of the three furnaces at a time. One would suppose that the capacity of the oxygen plant will be expanded to provide sufficient capacity for injection of oxygen to all eight furnaces.

Unit Cost of Inputs

Columns of unit cost information for the inputs to both pig iron and ingot steel production are shown in Table B.3. No information is shown

TABLE B.3 UNIT COST OF INPUTS

Inputs (in metric tons except where noted)	COSIPA July 1964 U.S. Dollars Per Unit	USIMINAS Jan. 1963 U.S. Dollars Per Unit
Regular iron ore	5.69	2.84
Iron ore fines	—	2.27
Sinter	11.70	5.54
Regular scrap	23.10	32.20
National coal	25.60	29.90
Imported coal	21.00	18.35
Coke	33.00	35.10
Limestone	4.61	5.04
Manganese	42.30	—
Fuel oil	27.60	—
Oxygen (1000 m³)*	—	40.00
Electrical energy (1000 kwh)	16.70	14.00
Water (1000 m³)	6.05	0.17
Steam	3.60	—
Steel shop refractories	117.00	—
Blast furnace gas (1000 m³)	2.18	—
Coke gas (1000 m³)	12.60	—
Exchange rate: cruzeiros per U.S. dollar	1300.00	475.00

* One thousand cubic meters.

for CSN because the only data available on unit cost for the inputs of the Volta Redonda plant of that firm are contained in a study, not yet released, of the Economic Commission for Latin America. The estimates used in this study for specific input cost at Volta Redonda are based on the ECLA study and on the information on input cost collected by the author at the COSIPA and USIMINAS plants.

The data for the COSIPA plant were provided by officials of that company and were given in cruzeiros of July 1964. In this table the data have been converted to cost in U.S. dollars per unit using the free market exchange rate of 1300 cruzeiros per U.S. dollar that prevailed in July 1964.

The data for USIMINAS were also provided by officials of that firm.

The information provided was in cruzeiros of January 1963. Consequently these data were converted to U.S. dollars at the free market exchange rate of 475 cruzeiros per U.S. dollar that held in January of 1963.

Since price indices on each of the types of inputs were not available, no attempt was made to deflate the data in cruzeiros to a common base before converting it to dollars.

Part II. A Set of Specific Inputs and Unit Cost of Inputs

Specific Inputs

This section and the next consist of descriptions of the specific inputs and unit cost used in the model for calculating pig iron and ingot steel cost at each of the plants.

A set of specific inputs for the production of pig iron and ingot steel in the three major plants in Brazil is shown in Tables B.4 and B.5. This

TABLE B.4 SPECIFIC INPUTS: PIG IRON
  (units per ton of product)

Input (in metric tons except where noted)	COSIPA	USIMINAS	CSN
Regular iron ore	0.700	0.470	0.782
Sinter	0.760	1.100	0.794
National coal	—	0.371	0.461
Imported coal	—	0.552	0.589
Coke	0.680	—	—
Dolomite	—	0.035	0.035
Limestone	0.400	0.132	0.272
Manganese	0.025	0.040	0.018
Fuel oil	—	—	0.050
Electrical energy (1000 kwh)	0.007	0.070	0.070
Water (1000 m³)*	0.650	0.100	0.015
Steam	0.020	—	—
Blast furnace gas (1000 m³)	−3.300	−2.624	−2.624
Coke gas (1000 m³)	−.138	−.138	−.138
Slag	−.430	−.476	−.476
Direct labor (man-hours)	0.390	0.390	0.390
Indirect labor (man-hours)	0.650	0.650	0.650
Maintenance (units)†	2.700	2.700	2.700

* One thousand cubic meters.
† Maintenance units (defined as $1 of maintenance cost).

set, which was used for most of the runs of the model, is based on information obtained from the publications of the Instituto Latinoameri-

TABLE B.5 SPECIFIC INPUTS: INGOT STEEL
(units per ton of product)

Input (in metric tons except where noted)	COSIPA	USIMINAS	CSN
Regular iron ore	0.040	0.005	0.111
Scrap	0.220	0.187	0.276
Plant scrap	—	0.014	0.039
Pig iron — liquid	0.880	0.929	0.628
Pig iron — ingots	0.016	—	0.097
Dolomite	—	0.006	—
Limestone	0.080	0.001	0.042
Quicklime	0.080	0.059	—
Aluminum	0.004	—	—
Fluorspar	0.008	0.004	—
Ferromanganese	0.007	—	—
Ferrosilicon	0.001	—	—
Fuel oil	—	—	0.118
Oxygen (1000 m^3)*	0.057	0.050	0.004
Electrical energy (1000 kwh)	0.022	0.012	—
Water (1000 m^3)	0.016	0.029	0.020
Steel furnace refractories	0.009	0.007	0.043
Direct labor (man-hours)	1.980	1.980	0.167
Indirect labor (man-hours)	—	—	0.950
Maintenance (units)†	4.500	4.500	6.340

* One thousand cubic meters.
† Maintenance units (defined as $1 of maintenance cost).

cano del Fierro y el Acero, ILAFA (the Latin American Iron and Steel Institute);[1] some studies of the Economic Commission for Latin America, ECLA;[2] annual reports of the steel companies; and data collected by the author while visiting eleven of the major steel mills in Latin America during the latter half of 1964 and the first month of 1965. These tables are based on the raw data contained in Part I of this appendix.

[1] See *Repertorio de las empress siderúrgicas latinoamericanas, 1962–1963,* published by ILAFA, Casilla 13810, Santiago, Chile, 1962. A new edition of this report that gives names of officials of the companies, descriptions of equipment, capacities, and production is published every two years. Also, see the monthly magazine of this organization, *Revista latinoamericana de siderurgia,* and a study done jointly by ILAFA and ECLA and sponsored by the Interamerican Development Bank, *Economía siderúrgica latinoamericana,* in particular the *Monografías nacionales* published by ILAFA in Santiago in 1963.

[2] ECLA, *Economía siderúrgica latinoamericana, op. cit.* Also, United Nations, Interregional Symposium on the Application of Modern Technical Practices in the Iron and Steel Industry to Developing Countries, "The Iron and Steel Industry of Latin America, Plans and Perspectives," Steel Symposium 1963/Discussion Paper/ECLA 2, 30 October 1963.

Some comments on the data in Tables B.4 and B.5 are in order at this point. The vectors of input coefficients for the COSIPA plant near Santos were those anticipated by the engineers, because neither the blast furnace nor the LD converters were yet in operation in January 1965. With the exception of the labor and maintenance inputs and the coke gas output, the data came from engineering studies prepared by the firm and by consultants for the firm. The labor and maintenance cost inputs came from the ECLA[3] study, and the coke gas output statistic came from a study on the Mexican steel industry mentioned earlier.[4] The blast furnace at the COSIPA plant was not equipped initially for fuel oil injection, which explains the coke rate of 680 kilograms per ton. Once the furnace is modified to permit fuel oil injection one would expect this coefficient to decrease by about 100 kilograms per ton or more, while the fuel oil coefficient will increase to between 50 and 100 kilograms per ton. It appears that there was an error in the COSIPA estimate of the specific input of water per ton of pig iron: for no apparent reason this estimate was much larger than for the other two plants. The original COSIPA estimate was used for the linear programming model but modified before runs were begun with the mixed-integer programming model.

The USIMINAS data reflect the actual operating conditions in the plant in the months prior to January 1965. At that time only one of the two blast furnaces was in operation and the plant was using a 100 per cent sinter charge. The data shown here assume that both blast furnaces are in operation. A vector of input coefficients for the one blast furnace operating with a 100 per cent sinter charge is shown in Part I of this appendix.

The coke input for the USIMINAS blast furnace has been divided into input coefficients for national and imported coal. The coke rate was 600 kilograms — the low rate resulting from the high sinter charge even without fuel injection. Sinter has some fuel mixed with it: therefore the lower rates. The labor and maintenance input coefficients for all plants come from the ECLA study cited earlier and are based on the operating experience of the Volta Redonda plant in 1962. Thus they provide a very rough approximation. Fortunately labor costs are not an important share of total cost in pig iron and ingot steel production. While technical information on raw materials inputs can be readily obtained, the equivalent information on labor input is often more closely held, so that representative data had to be used.

As in the case of COSIPA, the coke gas output coefficient was taken

[3] ECLA, *Economía siderúrgica latinoamericana, op. cit.,* Chapter 7.
[4] Comite para la programación de la industria siderúrgica, *Programación del desarrollo de la industria de aceros comunes laminador* (Mexico, D.F.: Nacional Financiera, November 1964), Vol. II, Appendix XIII.

from the Mexican study already mentioned. The same is true for the blast furnace gas coefficient. The dolomite input coefficient may be classified as an author's guess.

The CSN input vectors are based on information taken from flow charts for the operation of the plant in 1962. However, some modifications have been made. The estimated coke rate for the blast furnaces at Volta Redonda in 1962 was 764 kilograms per ton of pig iron. Since that date fuel oil injection equipment has been installed. Thus, it is assumed here that 50 kilograms of fuel oil is being injected per ton of pig iron produced, and that this injection has brought the coke rate down to 686 kilograms per ton of pig iron. Table B.4 shows the national and imported coal inputs required to produce 686 kilograms of coke. Modification of the other coefficients that may have occurred as a result of the injection has not been attempted here.

As with the other two plants, the gas output coefficients were taken from the Mexican experience and the labor and maintenance input coefficients from the ECLA study. Since the ECLA statistics on labor input came from a survey conducted in 1962 at Volta Redonda, they offer a reasonable approximation to the operating situation in the plant.

The specific input coefficients for ingot steel production shown in Table B.5 came from the same sources as those described for the input coefficients for the production of pig iron. The exceptions to this rule were the labor and maintenance input coefficients. The statistics for CSN came from the ECLA study but those for COSIPA and USIMINAS did not. The 1.98 man-hours per ton of ingot steel at USIMINAS is a number obtained by the author at the plant. The 4.50 units of maintenance were estimated to be somewhat less than the 6.34 for the equivalent input at Volta Redonda, since USIMINAS is a new plant with LD converters instead of open-hearth furnaces. The direct labor and maintenance coefficients for COSIPA (also a new plant) are assumed equal to those for USIMINAS.

Except for cases such as that of the sinter charge at USIMINAS, these input coefficients do not change markedly with changes in the output level of the plant. At USIMINAS the sinter charge will decrease from the 100 per cent level now used to the level shown in Table B.4 as soon as the second blast furnace is brought into operation.

The input coefficients may not be affected strongly by the level of output in a plant but they do change significantly with modifications to the equipment. Because of the discrete nature of changes in technology, these changes require the replacement of a vector of specific inputs by a new vector. The facility with which these vectors can be changed, new cost calculations made, and the elements of the linear programming matrix revised, increases the usefulness of this type of model in studying the effects of technical changes. A series of tests with different technologies was conducted on this model.

Unit Cost of Inputs

Table B.6 gives the unit cost (delivered at the plant) of inputs used for most of the experiments conducted with the model. It has been assumed that the supply of these inputs is perfectly elastic at the prices shown.

TABLE B.6   UNIT COST OF INPUTS
   (*dollars per unit*)

Input (in metric tons except where noted)	COSIPA	USIMINAS	CSN
Regular iron ore	5.69	2.84	3.50
Iron ore fines	—	2.27	—
Sinter	11.70	5.54	9.00
Scrap	23.10	32.20	24.00
Plant scrap	25.00	35.00	26.00
Pig iron — liquid	34.45	30.48	38.15
Pig iron — ingots	31.00	27.43	34.34
National coal	25.60	29.90	27.00
Imported coal	21.00	18.35	22.00
Coke	29.85	30.65	31.85
Limestone	4.61	5.04	5.00
Quicklime	6.00	6.00	6.00
Manganese	42.30	35.00	35.00
Fluorspar	20.00	20.00	20.00
Ferromanganese	280.00	280.00	280.00
Ferrosilicon	344.00	344.00	344.00
Fuel oil	27.60	25.00	28.00
Oxygen (1000 m³)*	40.00	40.00	40.00
Electrical energy (1000 kwh)	16.70	14.00	16.00
Water (1000 m³)	6.05	5.00	5.00
Steam	3.60	3.60	3.60
Steel furnace refractories	117.00	117.00	117.00
Blast furnace gas (1000 m³)	2.18	1.50	1.50
Coke gas (1000 m³)	12.60	7.00	7.00
Direct labor (man-hours)	0.42	0.42	0.42
Indirect labor (man-hours)	0.50	0.50	0.50
Maintenance (units)†	1.00	1.00	1.00

* One thousand cubic meters.
† Maintenance units (defined as $1 of maintenance cost).

The unit cost vector for COSIPA is based on estimates of the company in 1964. The basic data were in cruzeiros of July 1964 and were therefore converted to dollars at the free exchange rate of that date: 1,300 cruzeiros per U.S. dollar. The data for USIMINAS were for January 1963 and were in cruzeiros of that date. Therefore, they were converted to dollars at the free exchange rate of 475 cruzeiros per U.S. dollar. The data for CSN were estimated by the author on the basis of the unit cost for inputs at USIMINAS and COSIPA and a knowledge of the source of the raw materials used at Volta Redonda. Labor and maintenance cost estimates were taken from the ECLA study already mentioned.

The cost of coke inputs at the different plants was calculated as a weighted average of the cost of national and imported coals delivered at the plant. The weights employed were the percentage of national and imported coals used in each of the plants. In 1962 both COSIPA and USIMINAS used 40 per cent national and 60 per cent imported coal, while CSN used 44 per cent national and 56 per cent imported coal.[5]

Because of the tendency of most steel companies to prohibit the release of any cost information, it is difficult to obtain this kind of data.

TABLE B.7 COST BREAKDOWN IN DOLLARS PER TON OF PIG IRON

Input	COSIPA	USIMINAS	CSN
Regular iron ore	3.98	1.33	2.73
Sinter	8.89	6.09	7.14
National coal	—	11.09	12.44
Imported coal	—	10.12	12.95
Coke	20.30	—	—
Limestone	1.84	0.66	1.36
Manganese	1.05	1.40	0.63
Fuel oil	—	—	1.40
Electrical energy	0.11	0.98	1.12
Water	3.93	0.50	0.07
Steam	0.07	—	—
Blast furnace gas	−7.19	−3.93	−3.93
Coke gas	−1.73	−.96	−.96
Direct labor	0.16	0.16	0.16
Indirect labor	0.32	0.32	0.32
Maintenance	2.70	2.70	2.70
Total	34.45	30.48	38.15

For planning models of this sort one needs not only observations on the present cost of inputs (and better yet, some measure of the variability of these costs) but also some projections about how these costs may be expected to change over the time period included in the study.

[5] This information was obtained by the author in interviews at the steel plants and company offices.

The state of data availability in Brazil limits one to present (or recent past) prices in the form of single observations, without an indication of the variation of the prices. This situation is made more difficult by inflation. While one can deflate data obtained for different time periods or can use the free market exchange rate, these measures assume that there is no change in the relative prices of inputs to iron and steel production.

Difficulties of the type described suggest that it is wise to use the results of present planning models with care — but not to abstain from building the models. The data are improving and can be used with increasing confidence. More important, the models provide insight into the relative importance of different types of data. It may be that labor cost is such a small part of total cost in the steel industry and so stable over time that relatively rough measures may be used, while coal costs are so volatile and vary so much from location to location that detailed study of them is very important. Furthermore, it may be that distances between plants are so great that even relatively large variations in cost would not affect competitive positions in key market areas. The same holds true for variations in rates of exchange. It may be that rates of exchange vary so much that economic studies across national boundaries are useless. But this is something that one cannot be sure about until

TABLE B.8   COST BREAKDOWN IN DOLLARS PER TON OF INGOT STEEL

Input	COSIPA	USIMINAS	CSN
Regular iron ore	0.22	0.01	0.38
Scrap	5.08	6.02	6.62
Plant scrap	—	0.49	1.01
Pig iron — liquid	30.32	28.31	23.96
Pig iron — ingots	0.49	—	3.33
Limestone	0.36	—	0.21
Quicklime	0.48	0.35	—
Fluorspar	0.16	0.08	—
Ferromanganese	1.96	—	—
Ferrosilicon	0.34	—	—
Fuel oil	—	—	3.30
Oxygen	2.28	2.00	0.16
Electrical energy	0.36	0.16	—
Water	0.09	0.14	0.10
Steel furnace refractories	1.05	0.81	5.03
Direct labor	0.83	0.83	0.07
Indirect labor	—	—	0.47
Maintenance	4.50	4.50	6.34
Total	48.56	43.74	51.01

one knows how closely competitive the plants in various countries will be for market areas in one or the other country, until one knows something about the variation in exchange rates, and until one can test the stability of investment study models within the limits of the variations that are known to take place.

The cost breakdowns given in Tables B.7, B.8, and B.9 provide a

TABLE B.9   PRODUCTION COSTS
  (*U.S. dollars per metric ton*)

	Plate	Hot Sheet and Strip	Cold Sheet and Strip	Tin Plate
COSIPA	62.17	60.22	63.63	67.98
USIMINAS	55.99	54.25	57.30	61.23
CSN	65.29	63.25	66.82	71.41

measure of the relative importance of the different inputs in determining the total cost of pig iron, ingot steel, and other products.

Appendix C

The Single-Period Matrix

In this appendix the single-period model is presented with an accompanying discussion.

A list of the abbreviations used in the linear programming matrix is given in Table C.1, and the matrix itself is shown in Figure C.1. A brief introduction to the problem is followed by an explanation of each group of columns and rows in the matrix.

TABLE C.1 ABBREVIATIONS USED IN THE LINEAR PROGRAMMING MATRIX

Abbreviation	Explanation
SA	COSIPA plant near Santos
US	USIMINAS plant near Ipatinga
VR	CSN plant near Volta Redonda
SP	Market area around São Paulo
RJ	Market area around Rio de Janeiro
BH	Market area around Belo Horizonte
S	Product index for ingot steel
P	Product index for steel plate
H	Product index for hot sheet and strip
C	Product index for cold sheet and strip
T	Product index for tin plate
S	Steel furnaces
P	Primary rolling mill
R	Roughing mill
H	Hot strip finishing mill
C	Cold strip mill
T	Tinning line

The matrix consists of an objective row "Cost," thirty other rows, and sixty-six columns. The columns fall into four groups. The first of these is the set of activities for producing ingot steel at one plant and shipping it to another plant. The second group covers production-transportation

118

activities such as SASPP, that is, the production of steel plate at the Santos plant and its shipment to the market area of São Paulo. The third and fourth groups cover, respectively, imports and exports.

The rows may be divided into three groups. The first group consists of a single row, which is the objective row "Cost." The second group of rows is the set of production constraint rows, which prevents the output of each of the production units from exceeding its capacity. The last group of rows requires that the total production and transportation of products to each market area be at least sufficient to supply the requirements for each good.

The first six columns of the matrix are activity vectors for the production of ingot steel in one plant and its shipment to another plant as an intermediate product. For example, SAUSS (Column 1) is the activity name for the production of ingot steel at Santos and its delivery to the USIMINAS plant at Ipatinga. The cost of this activity is $18.54 per metric ton. This is equal to the cost of producing a ton of ingot steel at Santos, minus the cost of producing a ton of ingot steel at USIMINAS, plus the cost of transporting the ton of ingot steel from Santos to USIMINAS. This is the net cost to the system of this shipment of intermediate product.

Proceeding down the first column one finds 1.00 in the SAS row. This means that when activity SAUSS is operated at level x_1, then $(1.00) (x_1)$ units of the available steel capacity at Santos are used up. Thus, if $x_1 = .150$, then 150 thousand metric tons of ingot steel are produced at Santos and shipped to USIMINAS, thereby reducing the quantity of steel available for producing final products at Santos by 150 thousand tons. The right-hand side of the matrix shows that the constraint for the SAS row is the minimum of $(.72)/(.88)$ and $(.80)$. This requires that the ingot steel used for shipment to other plants and for use in final products, whether consumed domestically or exported, must be less than the minimum of the steel-equivalent capacity of the blast furnace or furnaces and the capacity of the steel shop. The capacity of the blast furnace at Santos is 720 thousand tons, and the specific input of pig iron to ingot steel production is 880 kilograms of pig iron per ton of ingot steel. The capacity of the LD converters in the steel shop is 800 thousand tons per year.

Returning to Column 1 of the matrix we encounter a value of -1 in the USS row. This means that each ton of ingot steel shipped from Santos to USIMINAS decreases by one unit the constraint on steel capacity at USIMINAS.

The remaining five columns of this group (Columns 2–6) repeat the pattern of Column 1 for each possible combination of shipping and receiving plant, with $+1$ in the row for the steel shop of the shipping plant and -1 in the row for the steel shop of the receiving plant.

FIGURE C.1. *The linear programming matrix.*

	1 SAUSS	2 SAVRS	3 USSAS	4 USVRS	5 VRSAS	6 VRUSS	7 SASPP	8 SARJP	9 SABHP	10 USSPP	11 USRJP	12 USBHP	13 VRSPP	14 VRRJP
0 COST	18.54	6.63	8.90	2.90	11.52	17.43	64.82	68.54	70.32	63.71	62.27	59.29	69.56	68.22
1 SAS	1.00	1.00	−1.00		−1.00		1.28	1.28	1.28					
2 SAP							1.28	1.28	1.28					
3 SAR							1.10	1.10	1.10					
4 SAH														
5 SAC														
6 SAT														
7 USS	−1.00		1.00	1.00		−1.00				1.28	1.28	1.28		
8 USP										1.28	1.28	1.28		
9 USR										1.10	1.10	1.10		
10 USH														
11 USC														
12 UST														
13 VRS		−1.00		−1.00	1.00	1.00							1.28	1.28
14 VRP													1.28	1.28
15 VRR													1.10	1.10
16 VRH														
17 VRC														
18 VRT														
19 SPP							1.00			1.00			1.00	
20 SPH														
21 SPC														
22 SPT														
23 RJP								1.00			1.00			1.00
24 RJH														
25 RJC														
26 RJT														
27 BHP									1.00			1.00		
28 BHH														
29 BHC														
30 BHT														

Figure C.1 (continued)

		15 VRBHP	16 SASPH	17 SARJH	18 SABHH	19 USSPH	20 USRJH	21 USBHH	22 VRSPH	23 VRRJH	24 VRBHH	25 SASPC	26 SARJC	27 SABHC	28 USSPC
0	COST	70.40	62.87	66.59	68.38	61.97	60.52	57.54	67.52	66.18	68.36	66.27	69.99	71.78	65.03
1	SAS		1.24	1.24	1.24							1.31	1.31	1.31	1.31
2	SAP		1.24	1.24	1.24							1.31	1.31	1.31	1.31
3	SAR		1.09	1.09	1.09							1.15	1.15	1.15	1.15
4	SAH		1.05	1.05	1.05							1.12	1.12	1.12	1.12
5	SAC											1.03	1.03	1.03	1.03
6	SAT														
7	USS					1.24	1.24	1.24							
8	USP					1.24	1.24	1.24							
9	USR					1.09	1.09	1.09							
10	USH					1.05	1.05	1.05							
11	USC														
12	UST														
13	VRS	1.28							1.24	1.24	1.24				
14	VRP	1.28							1.24	1.24	1.24				
15	VRR	1.10							1.09	1.09	1.09				
16	VRH								1.05	1.05	1.05				
17	VRC														
18	VRT														
19	SPP														
20	SPH		1.00			1.00			1.00						
21	SPC											1.00			1.00
22	SPT														
23	RJP														
24	RJH			1.00			1.00			1.00					
25	RJC												1.00		
26	RJT														
27	BHP	1.00													
28	BHH				1.00			1.00			1.00				
29	BHC													1.00	
30	BHT														

121

Figure C.1 (continued)

	29 USRJC	30 USBHC	31 VRSPC	32 VRRJC	33 VRBHC	34 SASPT	35 SARJT	36 SABHT	37 USSPT	38 USRJT	39 USBHT	40 VRSPT	41 VRRJT	42 VRBHT
0 COST	63.58	60.60	71.09	69.75	71.93	70.64	74.36	76.15	68.96	67.52	64.54	75.68	74.35	76.52
1 SAS						1.40	1.40	1.40						
2 SAP						1.40	1.40	1.40						
3 SAR						1.23	1.23	1.23						
4 SAH						1.20	1.20	1.20						
5 SAC						1.11	1.11	1.11						
6 SAT						1.05	1.05	1.05						
7 USS	1.31	1.31							1.40	1.40	1.40			
8 USP	1.31	1.31							1.40	1.40	1.40			
9 USR	1.15	1.15							1.23	1.23	1.23			
10 USH	1.12	1.12							1.20	1.20	1.20			
11 USC	1.03	1.03							1.11	1.11	1.11			
12 UST									1.05	1.05	1.05			
13 VRS			1.31	1.31	1.31							1.40	1.40	1.40
14 VRP			1.31	1.31	1.31							1.40	1.40	1.40
15 VRR			1.15	1.15	1.15							1.23	1.23	1.23
16 VRH			1.12	1.12	1.12							1.20	1.20	1.20
17 VRC			1.03	1.03	1.03							1.11	1.11	1.11
18 VRT												1.05	1.05	1.05
19 SPP														
20 SPH														
21 SPC			1.00											
22 SPT						1.00			1.00			1.00		
23 RJP														
24 RJH														
25 RJC	1.00			1.00										
26 RJT							1.00			1.00			1.00	
27 BHP														
28 BHH														
29 BHC		1.00			1.00									
30 BHT								1.00			1.00			1.00

122

Figure C.1 (continued)

		43 IMSPP 102.	44 IMSPH 102.	45 IMSPC 112.	46 IMSPT 122.	47 IMRJP 100.	48 IMRJH 100.	49 IMRJC 110.	50 IMRJT 120.	51 IMBHP 108.	52 IMBHH 108.	53 IMBHC 118.	54 IMBHT 128.	55 SAEXP −2.00	56 USEXP −2.00
0	COST														
1	SAS														
2	SAP													1.28	
3	SAR													1.28	
4	SAH													1.10	
5	SAC														
6	SAT														
7	USS														
8	USP														1.28
9	USR														1.28
10	USH														1.10
11	USC														
12	UST														
13	VRS														
14	VRP														
15	VRR														
16	VRH														
17	VRC														
18	VRT														
19	SPP	1.00													
20	SPH		1.00												
21	SPC			1.00											
22	SPT				1.00										
23	RJP					1.00									
24	RJH						1.00								
25	RJC							1.00							
26	RJT								1.00						
27	BHP									1.00					
28	BHH										1.00				
29	BHC											1.00			
30	BHT												1.00		

123

Figure C.1 (continued)

	57 VREXP	58 SAEXH	59 USEXH	60 VREXH	61 SAEXC	62 USEXC	63 VREXC	64 SAEXT	65 USEXT	66 VREXT		RHS
0 COST	−2.00	−3.00	−3.00	−3.00	−4.00	−4.00	−4.00	−5.00	−5.00	−5.00	≤	min $[\tfrac{1}{880}(.72),\ 0.80]$
1 SAS		1.24			1.31			1.40			≤	1.80
2 SAP		1.24			1.31			1.40			≤	1.00
3 SAR		1.09			1.15			1.23			≤	1.50
4 SAH		1.05			1.12			1.20			≤	.35
5 SAC					1.03			1.11			≤	.00
6 SAT								1.05			≤	min $[\tfrac{1}{525}(.90),\ 0.60]$
7 USS			1.24			1.31			1.40		≤	1.80
8 USP			1.24			1.31			1.40		≤	1.00
9 USR			1.09			1.15			1.23		≤	1.50
10 USH			1.05			1.12			1.20		≤	.15
11 USC						1.03			1.11		≤	.00
12 UST									1.05		≤	min $[\tfrac{1}{628}(1.00) - .15,\ 1.62 - .20]$
13 VRS	1.28			1.24			1.31			1.40	≤	1.40
14 VRP	1.28			1.24			1.31			1.40	≤	1.25
15 VRR	1.10			1.09			1.15			1.23	≤	1.50
16 VRH				1.05			1.12			1.20	≤	.80
17 VRC							1.03			1.11	≤	.28
18 VRT										1.05	≤	.02
19 SPP											≥	.20
20 SPH											≥	.30
21 SPC											≥	.15
22 SPT											≥	.16
23 RJP											≥	.12
24 RJH											≥	.16
25 RJC											≥	.06
26 RJT											≥	.02
27 BHP											≥	.08
28 BHH											≥	.14
29 BHC											≥	.04
30 BHT											≥	

124

Column 7 begins the second group of activity vectors. This group includes Columns 7 through 42 and contains an activity vector for the shipment to each of the three market areas from each of the three plants for each of the four final products, and thus includes (3)(3)(4), or 36 activity vectors.

The first vector SASPP (Column 7) is for the production of steel plate at Santos and its shipment to São Paulo. Thus, $64.82 is the cost per ton for the production and transportation of the product. The coefficient of 1.28 in the SAS row means that for each ton of steel plate produced at Santos, 1.28 tons of ingot steel are required. Similarly, the 1.28 in the second row SAP indicates that 1.28 tons of capacity in the primary mill at Santos are required for each ton of steel plate that is shipped. Likewise, before it is finished and ready for shipping the plate must pass through the roughing mill, but by the time the product reaches the roughing mill most of the scrap losses have already occurred. Therefore, only 1.10 tons of annual capacity at the roughing mill are required for each ton of plate.

Returning to the matrix, we find that the capacity of the primary mill at Santos is 1.80 million tons per year and the capacity of the roughing mill is 1.00 million tons per year. It is interesting to observe the variation in the capacity of the five main production units at the new steel plant at Santos. The steel equivalent capacity of the blast furnace is slightly more than 800 thousand tons per year, the capacity of the steel shop is 800 thousand tons, of the primary mill 1.80 million tons, of the roughing mill 1.00 million tons, and of the finishing mill 1.50 million tons. A part of this variation is because each of these units is required to process different amounts of product, even in a facility that is using all of them at capacity. However, a much more significant part of the variation is due to the technology of the equipment. The high capacity of the primary mill results from the fact that the economies of scale in the investment cost of this type of mill are strong up to capacities in this range. The same is true for the finishing mill but not for the roughing mill, where it is possible to install more stands as they are needed to increase the capacity. For the blast furnace and steel shop marginal investments can be made to increase substantially the present capacities. It is only mentioned here to point out why it is essential in a steel mill study to have a constraint row for each of the main production units and to think of investment as breaking first one bottleneck and then another or as breaking two or three bottlenecks simultaneously.

In Column 7 of the matrix there is a coefficient of 1.00 in Row 19. This row is in the group which requires that any solution to the problem be one for which the requirements of each market area for each product are satisfied. In this row, SPP (the annual requirement for plate in São

Paulo), there are coefficients of 1.00 in Columns 10 and 13. These two activities are also for the shipment of steel plate to São Paulo, the first being for shipments from USIMINAS and the second for shipments from Volta Redonda. The only other entry in this row is in Column 43; it is for the importation of plate to São Paulo. The value of the right-hand side for this constraint (Figure C.1) is .02. Thus, the annual requirement for steel plate in the São Paulo market area is 20 thousand tons, and this requirement must be fulfilled by shipments from some combination of the three plants and by imports.

Columns 7 through 9 are activity vectors for the production and shipment of steel plate from Santos to each of the three market areas, São Paulo, Rio de Janeiro, and Belo Horizonte. Columns 10 through 12 and 13 through 15 are for shipments of plate from USIMINAS and from Volta Redonda, respectively.

Column 16, SASPH, for the shipment of hot strip and sheets from Santos to São Paulo differs only slightly from Column 7. The scrap losses for hot sheet and strip are slightly less than for steel plate, so the first three coefficients in the column (after the objective function value) are slightly less than the corresponding values in Column 7. Also, there is the addition of a fourth coefficient. This is in row SAH, which is the capacity row for the hot strip finishing mill at Santos. Plate is not required to pass through the hot strip finishing mill, but hot strip and sheets are required to pass through this mill; therefore, the row SAH includes the coefficient shown.

Columns 16 through 24 are the activity vectors for the production and transportation of hot sheet and strip, and Columns 25 through 33 and 34 through 42 are the equivalent vectors for cold sheet and strip and for tin plate.

The third group of columns (Columns 43–54) gives the activity vectors for the importation of steel products. There is one activity vector for each product for each market, or $(4)(3) = 12$.

The last group of activity vectors (Columns 55–66) includes one vector for the export of each of the four products from each of the three plants. The coefficients within the matrix are the same as those for the vectors for production for domestic consumption. The objective function coefficients have been assigned negative values. Thus, exports are treated simply as a means of decreasing the total cost in the system. These values are the per unit profit for export activities and have greater absolute value for products that require more processing. For the same product the profit to be gained by each firm is assumed to be the same.

Appendix D

Transportation and Cost Data for the Mixed-Integer Programming Model

TABLE D.1 TRANSPORTATION COST: PLANTS TO MARKETS
(*U.S. dollars per ton*)

Plant	Market	Route	Transportation Cost
COSIPA	São Paulo	1	2.66
COSIPA	Rio de Janeiro	2	6.37
COSIPA	Belo Horizonte	2	8.16
USIMINAS	São Paulo	2	7.72
USIMINAS	Rio de Janeiro	2	6.28
USIMINAS	Belo Horizonte	2	3.30
CSN	São Paulo	2	4.27
CSN	Rio de Janeiro	1	2.94
CSN	Belo Horizonte	2	5.11

TABLE D.2 DISTANCES BETWEEN PLANTS AND MARKETS

Plant	Market	Route	Truck Train (kilometers)		Barge Ship (nautical miles)	
COSIPA	São Paulo	1	85	—	—	—
COSIPA	São Paulo	2	—	85	—	—
COSIPA	Rio de Janeiro	1	5	—	—	—
COSIPA	Rio de Janeiro	2	—	582	—	—
COSIPA	Rio de Janeiro	3	5	—	220	—
COSIPA	Belo Horizonte	1	642	—	—	—
COSIPA	Belo Horizonte	2	—	837	—	—
USIMINAS	São Paulo	1	771	—	—	—
USIMINAS	São Paulo	2	—	846	—	—
USIMINAS	São Paulo	3	85	451	480	—
USIMINAS	Rio de Janeiro	1	667	—	—	—
USIMINAS	Rio de Janeiro	2	—	640	—	—
USIMINAS	Rio de Janeiro	3	—	451	260	—
USIMINAS	Belo Horizonte	1	214	—	—	—
USIMINAS	Belo Horizonte	2	—	214	—	—
CSN	São Paulo	1	353	—	—	—
CSN	São Paulo	2	—	353	—	—
CSN	Rio de Janeiro	1	146	—	—	—
CSN	Rio de Janeiro	2	—	252	—	—
CSN	Belo Horizonte	1	473	—	—	—
CSN	Belo Horizonte	2	—	473	—	—

TABLE D.3 TRANSPORTATION COST: PLANT TO PLANT
(U.S. dollars per ton)

From	To	Transportation Cost
COSIPA	USIMINAS	7.63
COSIPA	CSN	3.37
USIMINAS	COSIPA	7.63
USIMINAS	CSN	5.51
CSN	COSIPA	3.37
CSN	USIMINAS	5.51

TABLE D.4 DISTANCES BETWEEN PLANTS

From	To	Kilometers
COSIPA	USIMINAS	1300.00
COSIPA	CSN	430.00
USIMINAS	COSIPA	1300.00
USIMINAS	CSN	868.00
CSN	COSIPA	430.00
CSN	USIMINAS	868.00

TABLE D.5 PRODUCTION COST
   (*U.S. dollars per ton*)

Plant	Pig Iron	Ingots	Slabs	Plate	Hot Strip	Cold Strip	Tin Plate
COSIPA	31.97	46.34	51.07	57.95	62.00	72.91	125.00
USIMINAS	29.47	42.80	46.32	52.78	56.63	66.41	116.80
CSN	36.52	49.84	54.80	61.75	65.84	76.95	129.30

TABLE D.6 SPECIFIC INPUTS: PIG IRON

Input (in metric tons except where noted)	COSIPA	USIMINAS	CSN
Regular iron ore	.700	.470	.782
Sinter	.760	1.100	.794
National coal	—	.371	.461
Imported coal	—	.552	.589
Coke	.680	—	—
Dolomite	—	.035	.035
Limestone	.400	.132	.272
Manganese	.025	.040	.018
Fuel oil	—	—	.050
Electrical energy (1000 kwh)	.070	.070	.070
Water (1000 m³)*	.065	.100	.015
Steam	.020	—	—
Blast furnace gas (1000 m³)	−3.300	−3.300	−3.715
Coke gas (1000 m³)	−.138	−.138	−.138
Slag	−.430	−.476	−.476
Direct labor (man-hours)	.390	.390	.390
Indirect labor (man-hours)	.650	.650	.650
Maintenance (units)†	2.700	2.700	2.700

* One thousand cubic meters.
† Maintenance units (defined as $1 of maintenance cost).

TABLE D.7 SPECIFIC INPUTS: INGOT STEEL

Input (in metric tons except where noted)	COSIPA	USIMINAS	CSN
Regular iron ore	.040	.005	.111
Scrap	.220	.187	.276
Plant scrap	—	.014	.039
Pig iron — liquid	.880	.929	.628
Pig iron — ingots	.016	—	.097
Dolomite	—	.006	—
Limestone	.080	.001	.042
Quicklime	.080	.059	—
Aluminum	.004	—	—
Fluorspar	.008	.004	—
Ferromanganese	.007	—	—
Ferrosilicon	.001	—	—
Fuel oil	—	—	.118
Oxygen (1000 m³)*	.057	.050	.004
Electrical energy (1000 kwh)	.022	.012	—
Water (1000 m³)	.016	.029	.020
Steel furnace refractories	.009	.007	.043
Direct labor (man-hours)	1.980	1.980	.167
Indirect labor (man-hours)	—	—	.950
Maintenance (units)†	4.500	4.500	6.340

* One thousand cubic meters.
† Maintenance units (defined as $1 of maintenance cost).

TABLE D.8 UNIT COST OF INPUTS
(U.S. dollars per unit)

Input (in metric tons except where noted)	COSIPA	USIMINAS	CSN
Regular iron ore	5.69	2.84	3.50
Iron ore fines	—	2.27	—
Sinter	11.70	5.54	9.00
Scrap	23.10	32.20	24.00
Plant scrap	25.00	35.00	26.00
Pig iron — liquid	31.97	29.47	36.52
Pig iron — ingots	28.77	26.52	32.87
National coal	25.60	29.90	27.00
Imported coal	21.00	18.35	22.00
Coke	29.85	30.66	31.86
Limestone	4.61	5.04	5.00
Quicklime	6.00	6.00	6.00
Manganese	42.30	35.00	35.00
Fluorspar	20.00	20.00	20.00
Ferromanganese	280.00	280.00	280.00
Ferrosilicon	344.00	344.00	344.00
Fuel oil	27.60	25.00	28.00
Oxygen (1000 m³)*	40.00	40.00	40.00
Electrical energy (1000 kwh)	16.70	14.00	16.00
Water (1000 m³)	6.05	5.00	5.00
Steam	3.60	3.60	3.60
Steel furnace refractories	117.00	117.00	117.00
Blast furnace gas (1000 m³)	2.18	1.50	1.50
Coke gas (1000 m³)	12.60	7.00	7.00
Direct labor (man-hours)	.42	.42	.42
Indirect labor (man-hours)	.50	.50	.50
Maintenance (units)†	1.00	1.00	1.00

* One thousand cubic meters.
† Maintenance units (defined as $1 of maintenance cost).

TABLE D.9   Cost Breakdown: U.S. Dollars per Ton of Pig Iron

Input	COSIPA	USIMINAS	CSN
Regular iron ore	3.98	1.33	2.74
Sinter	8.89	6.09	7.15
National coal	—	11.09	12.45
Imported coal	—	10.13	12.96
Coke	20.30	—	—
Limestone	1.84	.67	1.36
Manganese	1.06	1.40	.63
Fuel oil	—	—	1.40
Electrical energy	1.17	.98	1.12
Water	.39	.50	.07
Steam	.07	—	—
Blast furnace gas	−7.19	−4.95	−5.57
Coke gas	−1.74	−.97	−.97
Direct labor	.16	.16	.16
Indirect labor	.32	.32	.32
Maintenance	2.70	2.70	2.70
Total	31.97	29.47	36.52

TABLE D.10   Cost Breakdown: U.S. Dollars per Ton of Ingot Steel

Input	COSIPA	USIMINAS	CSN
Regular iron ore	.23	.01	.39
Scrap	5.08	6.02	6.62
Plant scrap	—	.49	1.01
Pig iron — liquid	28.13	27.38	22.94
Pig iron — ingots	.46	—	3.19
Limestone	.37	.01	.21
Quicklime	.48	.35	—
Fluorspar	.16	.08	—
Ferromanganese	1.96	—	—
Ferrosilicon	.34	—	—
Fuel oil	—	—	3.30
Oxygen	2.28	2.00	.16
Electrical energy	.37	.17	—
Water	.10	.14	.10
Steel furnace refractories	1.05	.82	5.03
Direct labor	.83	.83	.07
Indirect labor	—	—	.47
Maintenance	4.50	4.50	6.34
Total	46.34	42.80	49.84

Appendix E

Evidence on Equipment Cost

Steel companies and equipment manufacturing concerns so zealously guard information on equipment cost that the information that is publicly available is very limited. However, there are a number of places to search for the evidence.[1]

The Instituto Latinoamericano del Fierro y el Acero has recently made a survey of the major companies in Latin America to obtain information on equipment cost. Data from this survey are helpful for estimating costs of coke plants, blast furnaces, and oxygen converters but are too aggregative to be of any help in estimating the costs of rolling mills and other equipment.

The Wall Street Journal also provides some clues about equipment cost in the steel industry. However, the stories in this newspaper usually carry incomplete technical descriptions of the equipment and explain that the cost of the equipment was not announced by the company but that "industry sources" estimated what the amount was.

Also, some of the technical publications of the industry occasionally provide some cost information. The *Revista* of ILAFA and *Blast Furnace and Steel Plant* are two of the most helpful.

Studies by the United Nations, particularly by the Economic Commission for Europe and the Economic Commission for Latin America, also provide some information. However, the results of these studies are usually to give an equation of the form

$$C = aX^b$$

where C is the cost of the equipment, a is a constant, X is the annual capacity of the unit, and b is a constant such that $0 \leq b \leq 1$. The sources from which the data to estimate the function were obtained are vague, and the data are not usually published.

Finally, there are feasibility studies. These studies are always con-

[1] For reference citations see Table E.1.

133

TABLE E.1   Evidence on Equipment Cost for the Making of Steel and the Rolling of Flat Products

Unit Plant	Capacity (million metric tons per year)	Investment (millions of U.S. dollars)		Data Source
1. Coke Plant				
(a) A	.487	15.7		ILAFA
(b) B	.250	17.2		ILAFA
(c) COSIPA, Santos, Brazil		5.9[1]		Revista, No. 45, p. 15
(d) C (43 ovens, 15 tons each)	.220	13.9		ILAFA
(e) D		11.8		ILAFA
(f) Jones & Laughlin (59 ovens)	.360	6.0		WSJ, 12/1/58
(g) Bethlehem Steel (76 ovens)		7.5		WSJ, 12/15/59
(h) E (74 ovens)	.450	18.6		AID
2. Sinter Plant				
(a) Pittsburgh Steel, Monessen, Pa.	.500	3.5		WSJ, 3/6/62
(b) COSIPA, Santos, Brazil		4.4[1]		
(c) The experience of German plants:				
"small" plants				
— U.S.$13–14 per metric ton of capacity				UN Steel Symp., 1963
"large" plants				
— U.S.$11.5–12.5 per metric ton of capacity				Tech. Paper/A.7
3. Blast Furnaces				
(a) A	.515	23.7		ILAFA
(b) C	.220	12.4		ILAFA
(c) F	.450	12.0		ILAFA
(d) D (2 blast furnaces)	.464	9.4		ILAFA
(e) E	.440	13.2		AID
(f) G	1.220	43.7		
(g) Propulsora, La Plata, Arg. (P)	.635	20.0		Project Study
4. Oxygen Converters				
(a) B (2 LD's, 45 tons each, 2 mixers, 800 tons each)	.600	16.9		ILAFA
(b) F (2 LD's)	.500	20.0		ILAFA
(c) E (2 LD's, 80 tons each)	.470	15.3		AID
(d) G (2 LD's, 170 tons each)	1.400	51.4		
(e) G (first two vessels)	1.400	51.4	29.6[2]	
(add a third vessel)		13.0	7.5[2]	
(add a fourth and fifth)		39.5	23.1[2]	
(f) COSIPA (2 LD's)	.800	7.6+		Revista, No. 45, p. 15
(g) U.S. Steel, Gary, Ind. (3 LD's)		30.0		WSJ, 9/24/63
(h) National Steel, Weirton, Pa. (2 B.D.F.'s)	1.5–2.0	30.0		WSJ, 8/12/60
(i) Republic Steel (2 B.D.F.'s, 220 tons each)		40.0		WSJ, 3/25/64

TABLE E.1   (continued)

Unit Plant	Capacity (million metric tons per year)	Investment (millions of U.S. dollars)	Data Source
5. Oxygen Plants			
(a) COSIPA (for 2 LD converters with a capacity of 800 thousand metric tons per year)		2.6[1]	*Revista*, No. 45, p. 15
(b) Wheeling Steel Company	.150	6.0	*WSJ*, 6/18/59
6. Continuous Casting			
(a) F (slabs)	.200	4.0	
(bars)	.200	3.0	
(b) National Steel, Weirton, Pa. (4 stand low overhead, slabs up to 9″ thick by 40″ wide)	1.500	10.0	*WSJ*, 3/25/64 *NYT*, 3/18/64
7. Primary Mill			
(a) G (46″ x 90″ slabbing mill)	4.000	57.0	
(b) COSIPA, Santos, Brazil (44″ wide)	1.800	5.7[3]	*Revista*, No. 45, p. 15
8. Plate Mill			
(a) G (140″ wide plate mill)		82.0	
(b) COSIPA (110″ wide plate mill)		7.8[3]	*Revista*, No. 45, p. 15
9. Hot Strip Mills			
(a) Pittsburgh Steel (56″ wide)	1.7	45.0	*WSJ*, 5/15/59
(b) Republic Steel		55.0	*WSJ*, 6/23/60
(c) Jones & Laughlin, Cleveland, Ohio		60.0	*WSJ*, 11/18/61
(d) G (80″ wide)	3.5	92.0	
(e) COSIPA (66″ wide)	1.5	4.6[3]	*Revista*, No. 45, p. 15
(f) Armco, Middletown, Ohio	3.6	125.0	*BF&SP*, Jan. 1965, Vol. 53, p. 81
10. Cold Strip Mills			
(a) U.S. Steel Corp. (6 stand)		20.0	*WSJ*, 12/17/63
(b) Inland (54″, 3 stand, 5,000 ft per min, coils up to 48,000 lb)		5.0[4]	*WSJ*, 5/6/63
(c) Kaiser (3 stands for light tin plate)		15.0	*WSJ*, 3/25/64
(d) COSIPA, Santos, Brazil	.350	1.9[3]	*Revista*, No. 45, p. 15
(e) Propulsora, La Plata, Arg. (may include shearing line and/or pickling line)	.300	20.0	Project Study
11. Tinning Lines			
(a) F	.100	5.0	
(b) Kaiser Steel (thin tin plate, 3 stand)		15.0	*WSJ*, 6/13/63
(c) Republic Steel, Warren, Pa. (54″, 2 stand)		10.0	
		5.0[4]	*WSJ*, 5/6/63
(d) National, Weirton, Pa. (2 stand)		15.0	*WSJ*, 3/24/65

TABLE E.1   (continued)

Unit Plant	Capacity (million metric tons per year)	Investment (millions of U.S. dollars)	Data Source
12. Galvanizing Line			
(a) F	.100	3.0	
(b) Bethlehem, Calif. (54″ wide 400 to			
500 ft per min)	.280	20.0	BF&SP, Jan. 1965, Vol. 53, p. 59

Key to references:
ILAFA = unpublished survey by the Instituto Latinoamericano del Fierro y el Acero, "Inversiones siderurgicas latinoamericanas," Santiago, Chile, 1965.
Revista = *Revista Latinoamericana de siderurgia*, monthly magazine published by ILAFA.
WSJ = *The Wall Street Journal*.
UN Steel Symp. = United Nations, "Interregional Symposium on the Application of Modern Technical Practices in the Iron and Steel Industry to Developing Countries," 1963.
AID = The Agency for International Development, Washington, D.C.
NYT = *The New York Times*.
BF&SP = *Blast Furnace and Steel Plant*, monthly publication of Steel Publications, Inc.
[1] Equipment cost only, f.o.b.
[2] Equipment cost only, purchase price.
[3] Mechanical equipment only, f.o.b.
[4] Mechanical and electrical equipment only.

fidential, are difficult to obtain, and cannot be quoted. Also, the data they contain are expectations about what equipment costs will be rather than statements about what the costs were.

Table E.1 contains the evidence that the author was able to obtain. some of the companies are referred to with letters of the alphabet in order not to violate the confidence of the institutions that supplied the data. The investment cost given in the second column should be regarded as the cost of purchasing and installing the unit unless otherwise noted.

The estimates of capital costs for the projects included in the model were made on the basis of the information contained in Table E.1 and on some additional information that will be discussed in the section to follow.

The estimates of the cost of modifying the blast furnaces at COSIPA and USIMINAS to increase their productivity were based on estimates of the cost of modifying a large blast furnace in another Latin American country. Data from that estimate are shown in Table E.2. Though the blast furnace at COSIPA has just been installed and probably already contains some of the features in the list of modifications in Table E.2, it is assumed that all of the modifications could be added to the COSIPA blast furnace at a cost of $1.8 million with an increase in the capacity of the furnace from .720 to 1.000 million metric tons per year.

TABLE E.2   COST OF MODIFICATIONS TO A BLAST FURNACE: TOTAL COST DOMESTIC AND FOREIGN
(in thousands of U.S. dollars)

Modification	Cost
Increase top pressure	402.0
Humidity content	8.5
Addition of a fourth stove	
(25′ diam., 110′ high)	891.0
Injection of petroleum	200.0
Distribution of electrical energy	9.0
Parts	45.0
Engineering	50.0
Contingencies	160.0
Total	1,765.5

Since there are two blast furnaces at USIMINAS and space for one additional stove (to heat the blast air), it is assumed that the modification cost would be double for increasing the top pressure, and adding humidity control and the injection of petroleum, but that all other components of the cost would be as shown in Table E.2. Thus, it is assumed that the output of the two blast furnaces could be increased from a rated capacity of .900 to 1.260 million metric tons per year with an investment cost of $2.4 million.

To estimate the cost of investments for building new blast furnaces, Figure E.1 was constructed from the data in Table E.1. The letter on the points in the plot are for the corresponding plant name in the table. In addition there are two points labeled "Muller." These two points were calculated from the function

$$C = 40(x)^{.60},$$

where C is the capital cost for the investment in millions of U.S. dollars and x is the capacity of the blast furnace in millions of metric tons of pig iron per year. This function was taken from a study by Gunther Muller[2] based on an earlier study by the Economic Commission for Europe.[3]

[2] Gunther H. Muller, "Aspectos económicos del proceso HyL," ILAFA, Cuarto Congreso Latinoamericana de Siderurgia, Mexico City, D.F. 1964.
[3] United Nations, Economic Commission for Europe, A Comparison of Steel Making Processes, New York, 1962.

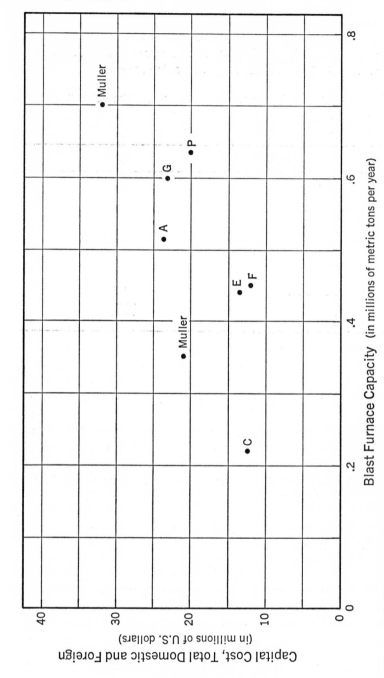

FIGURE E.1. *Blast furnace investment cost.*

In recent years a series of modifications in blast furnace design and operation have resulted in significant increases in the productivity of existing blast furnaces, and, one would suppose, in decreases in the cost per ton of capacity in new blast furnaces. For this reason greater weight should be given to points E and P in Figure E.1, as they represent projects recently completed or not yet begun while the other points in the graph represent blast furnaces of slightly greater vintage than F and P. With greatest weight given to the four points F, P, G, and E, and on the basis of a very rough projection, a cost of \$28 million is chosen as the capital cost for the installation of a blast furnace with a capacity of 800 thousand metric tons per year. Though there would be some differences in the cost of erecting a blast furnace of this size at the three different plants and there would be differences in the cost of capital to the different companies, these differences are assumed away in the model.

A plot of investment cost versus capacity for a pair of LD converters is shown in Figure E.2. As with the previous graph, the letters and names refer to plants listed in Table E.1. Muller's equation for converters is

$$C = 19.5(x)^{.71}.$$

The equation for the points marked ECLA is not given in the study.[4]

From Figure E.2, it appears that a fair guess for the capital cost of a pair of LD converters with a capacity of 800 thousand metric tons per year would be \$21 million. Since it is also often necessary to add to the infrastructure of the plant when new productive units are installed and since infrastructure investment in a new plant may account for almost half of the total investment, but will certainly be less in the usual addition to plant capacity, it is assumed that the total investment cost associated with the installation of a pair of LD converters of 800 thousand metric tons is 1.5 (\$21 million) = \$31.5 million.

Table E.1 shows that in the case of plant G, where plans were made for the installation of two LD converters, then a third, and then two more, the capital cost of the third LD was roughly one-fourth of the cost of the original pair and the cost of the final pair was about three-fourths of that of the original pair. If one accepts the cost of \$31.5 million for a pair of LD converters, this yields a cost of \$7.9 million for a third converter and a cost of \$23.6 for a fourth and fifth.

The scant data obtained on the cost of plate mills makes it difficult to estimate the cost of adding a stand to the existing reversing rougher at COSIPA. The cost of the 140-inch plate mill at plant G is shown by Table E.1 to have been estimated at \$82 million, and according to a report in

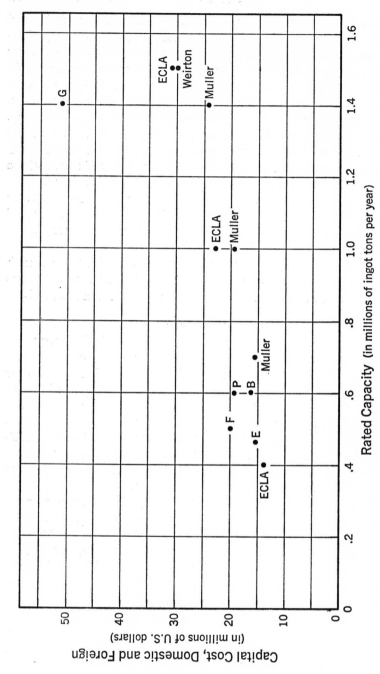

FIGURE E.2. *Investment cost of LD converters (2 LD converters).*

Revista (see Table E.1) the cost of the mechanical equipment alone of the 110-inch plate mill already installed at COSIPA was $7.8 million. So, taking a wild guess, it is assumed that the total cost of the equipment and the modifications required to increase the capacity of the roughing mill at COSIPA by one million metric tons from its present annual capacity of one million metric tons will be $25 million.

From the results shown in the appropriate sections of Table E.1, it is assumed that the cost of installing a cold strip mill of 350 thousand metric tons per year will be $10 million, and the cost of installing a tinning line of 180 thousand metric tons per year capacity will be $8 million.

Appendix F

Structure of the Matrix and the Right-Hand Side for the Multiperiod Model

Figure F.1 shows the structure of the mixed-integer programming model. The upper-case letters represent matrices, the boldface lower-case letters represent vectors, and the other lower-case letters represent elements. The superscripts on the variables show the time period. No time superscripts are placed on the matrices because it is assumed that the capacity utilization aspect of the technology remains constant over time.

There are three large vectors and one large matrix in Figure F.1.

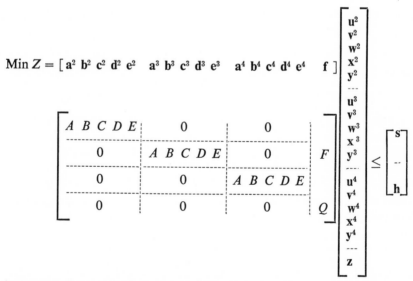

FIGURE F.1. *The multiperiod matrix and the right-hand side.*

The row vector just above the matrix is the vector of activity cost. Its component vectors $\mathbf{a}^2$, $\mathbf{b}^2$, $\mathbf{c}^2$, $\cdots$, represent the corresponding elements in the objective functions (Equation 3.6 on page 24). For example, the vector $\mathbf{b}^2$ is composed of the elements b_i^{k2}. The same is true of the column vector of unknowns; that is, the components of the vector $\mathbf{z}$ are z_r.

The right-hand-side vector is shown to the right of the inequality sign. It consists of the $\mathbf{s}$ vector, which contains elements for the capacity of each productive unit in each time period and elements for the requirement of each market area for each product in each time period. The $\mathbf{h}$ vector is the lower part of the right-hand side and contains elements used to constrain the investment variable to integer values.

The principal components of the matrix are the three stair steps and the F and Q matrices. The F matrix is the investment matrix, and the Q matrix is the integer constraint matrix. Each stair step consists of five matrices. The A matrix is for intermediate product shipments, the B matrix is for imports of intermediate products, the C matrix is for domestic production-transportation activities for final products, the D matrix is for imports of final products, and the E matrix is for exports of both intermediate and final products.

The structure of this matrix is in many aspects similar to the multi-time-period matrix used by Vietorisz in his fertilizer plant location study.[1]

The Elements of the Matrix and the Right-Hand Side

Figure F.2 shows the arangement of the matrices A_i in the A matrix. The notation at the top of the matrix (P_1P_2, P_1P_3, and so on), indicates the direction of product flow in that section of the matrix. For example, P_1P_2 is for shipments from plant 1 to plant 2. Thus, shipments from plant 1 to plant 2 use up capacity of the productive units in plant 1 (the elements of A_1 in this series of columns are positive), and they add to effective capacity in plant 2 (the elements of A_2 in this series of columns are negative). The elements of the matrices A_i are shown in Figure F.3.

The large zero in the bottom half of the A matrix indicates that inter-plant shipments of intermediate products have no effect on the satisfaction of final product requirements. The elements σ_t^{kj} in the vector $\mathbf{r}_t$ in the right-hand side are the requirements for market area j for final product k in the tth time period. The $\mathbf{k}$ vector is composed of elements γ_i^e,

[1] Thomas Vietorisz, "Industrial Development Planning Models with Economies of Scale and Indivisibilities," mimeo., IBM Thomas J. Watson Research Center, Yorktown Heights, N.Y., 1963.

Column headers:

P_1P_2 P_2P_1 P_2P_3 P_3P_1 P_3P_2 | IP_1 IP_2 IP_3 | P_1M_1 P_1M_2 P_1M_3 P_2M_1 P_2M_2 P_2M_3 P_3M_1 P_3M_2 P_3M_3 | IM_1 IM_2 IM_3 | EP_1 EP_2 EP_3

$$
\begin{bmatrix}
A_1 & -A_1 & 0 & -A_1 & 0 & -A_1 & & & & & & & & & & & & & & & A_1C_1 & & \\
-A_2 & 0 & A_2 & 0 & -A_2 & & -A_2 & & & & & & & & & & & & & & & A_2C_2 & \\
0 & -A_3 & 0 & A_3 & A_3 & & & -A_3 & & & & & & & & & & & & & & & A_3C_3 \\
 & & & & & & & & C_1 & C_1 & C_1 & & & & & & & -I_{12} & & & & & \\
 & & & & & & & & & & & C_2 & C_2 & C_2 & & & & & 0 & & & & \\
 & & & & & & & & & & & & & & C_3 & C_3 & C_3 & & & -I_{13} & & &
\end{bmatrix}
\leq
\begin{bmatrix} \mathbf{k} \\ -\mathbf{r} \end{bmatrix}
$$

Group labels (left to right):

A	B	C	D	E
Interplant shipments of intermediate products	Imports of intermediate products	Plant to market shipments of final products	Imports of final products	Exports of both intermediate and final products

FIGURE F.2. *The single-period submatrix.*

$$A_i = \begin{bmatrix} \alpha_i^{ke} \end{bmatrix}_{k=1,2,3} = \begin{bmatrix} \alpha_i^{11} & \alpha_i^{21} & \alpha_i^{31} \\ 0 & \alpha_i^{22} & \alpha_i^{32} \\ 0 & 0 & \alpha_i^{33} \\ 0 & 0 & 0 \\ 0 & 0 & 0 \\ 0 & 0 & 0 \\ 0 & 0 & 0 \\ 0 & 0 & 0 \end{bmatrix}$$

α_i^{ke} = metric tons of capacity required in production unit e of plant i for each metric ton of product k produced at plant i.

Intermediate Products

$$C_i = \begin{bmatrix} \alpha_i^{ke} \end{bmatrix}_{k=4,5,6,7} = \begin{bmatrix} \alpha_i^{41} & \alpha_i^{51} & \alpha_i^{61} & \alpha_i^{71} \\ \alpha_i^{42} & \alpha_i^{52} & \alpha_i^{62} & \alpha_i^{72} \\ \alpha_i^{43} & \alpha_i^{53} & \alpha_i^{63} & \alpha_i^{73} \\ \alpha_i^{44} & \alpha_i^{54} & \alpha_i^{64} & \alpha_i^{74} \\ 0 & \alpha_i^{55} & \alpha_i^{65} & \alpha_i^{75} \\ 0 & 0 & \alpha_i^{66} & \alpha_i^{76} \\ 0 & 0 & 0 & \alpha_i^{77} \end{bmatrix}$$

Final Products

FIGURE F.3. *The capacity utilization submatrices* A *and* C.

which give the capacity of productive unit e in plant i at the beginning of the time covered by the model.

The *B* matrix represents imports of intermediate products. The matrices A_i in the *B* matrix are identical to those in the *A* matrix (except for sign) and consist entirely of negative elements because all imports of intermediate products serve to ease capacity constraints. The notation IP_1 indicates that the series of columns in that section of the matrix are for imports of intermediate products to plant 1.

The next section of the matrix, the *C* matrix, is the familiar linear programming production-transportation problem. Figure F.3 shows that the elements of the matrices C_i are the metric tons of capacity required in productive unit e at plant i for each metric ton of final product k produced. The final products and productive units are

Product Indices		Productive-Unit Indices	
Index	Final Product	Index	Productive Unit
4	Steel plate	1	Blast furnace
5	Hot sheet and strip	2	Steel furnaces
6	Cold sheet and strip	3	Primary mill
7	Tin plate	4	Roughing mill
		5	Hot strip mill
		6	Cold strip mill
		7	Tinning line

The arrangement of the matrices C_i in the C matrix is shown in Figure F.2. The notation P_1M_1 indicates that the series of columns in this section of the matrix are for shipments of final products from plant 1 to market area 1. The subscripts on the identity matrices I indicate the number of rows and columns in these square matrices. Thus, the activities in the series of columns headed by P_1M_1 use up capacity in the productive units of plant 1 and at the same time satisfy the final-product requirements of market area 1. The negative sign on the identity matrices and on the lower portion of the right-hand-side vector $\mathbf{r}$ exist because all elements in these rows have been multiplied by minus one in order to reverse the inequality.

The D matrix represents the importation of final products. These activities affect only the satisfaction of market requirements.

The activities for exporting both intermediate and final products are included in the E matrix. The notation EP_i at the top of the matrix indicates that the activities in that section of the matrix are for the exportation of products from plant i. In the E matrix the submatrices A_i and C_i are placed side by side to create triangular matrices.

TABLE F.1   ABBREVIATIONS USED IN THE MULTIPERIOD MATRIX

Sources		
	SA	COSIPA plant near Santos
	US	USIMINAS plant near Ipatinga
	VR	CSN plant near Volta Redonda
	IM	Imports
Sinks		
	SP	São Paulo market area
	RJ	Rio de Janeiro market area
	BH	Belo Horizonte market area
	EX	Exports
Products		
	G	Pig iron
	S	Ingot steel
	L	Slabs
	P	Plate
	H	Hot sheet and strip
	C	Cold sheet and strip
	T	Tin plate
Productive Units		
	B	Blast furnace
	S	Steel shop
	P	Primary mill
	H	Hot strip mill
	C	Cold strip mill
	T	Tinning line

The abbreviations described in Table F.1 are helpful in reading Figure F.4, which is a picture of a print-out of the matrix for the second time period. This print-out of the matrix was made with a program that is part of the LP/11 system developed by Norman Driebeek of the Arthur D. Little Company. The legend gives the key to the magnitudes of the numbers shown in the picture.

Figure F.1 shows that the investment matrix F is appended to the right-hand side of the multiperiod model. The details of this matrix are shown in Figure F.5. The first third of the figure contains the rows for the second time period as well as the corresponding right-hand side. The last two thirds of the figure show the similar sections for periods 3 and 4.

The first seven rows of Figure F.5 represent the production units of the COSIPA steel mill at Santos (SA) near São Paulo. The second seven rows are for the USIMINAS (US) plant in Minas Gerais state, and the third group of seven rows are for the Volta Redonda (VR) plant of CSN located between Rio de Janeiro and São Paulo. The next four rows (22–25) are requirement rows for the market area of São Paulo (SP), and the eight final rows are the corresponding requirement rows for the market areas of Rio de Janeiro (RJ) and Belo Horizonte (BH). The map in Chapter 4 shows the location of these plants and market areas.

The same abbreviations are used to identify the twenty-three investment opportunities. Thus, the variable 2ISAS in the first column of the F matrix represents an investment in the steel furnaces at the plant at Santos. This project would be completed and ready to begin operation by the beginning of the second time period. Similarly, the variable 3IUSB represents an investment to be completed by the beginning of the third time period in the blast furnace at the USIMINAS plant.

The column RHS is for the right-hand side. The entries in the first 21 rows in this column (which make up the vector **k**) are the capacity of each productive unit in 1965. The entries in the last twelve rows of the RHS column (which make up the r_2 vector) reflect the market requirements in the second time period.

The entry of $-.80$ in row 2SAS and column 2ISAS indicates that the investment opportunity 2ISAS would add 800 thousand metric tons to the capacity of the steel shop in the Santos plant. In the same way, the project 2IVRT is for the installation of a tinning line with a capacity of 180 thousand metric tons of tin plate per year. The capacity of the existing electrolytic tin line at the Volta Redonda plant is 170 thousand metric tons per year, so the proposed investment would more than double the capacity of the tinning section of this steel mill.

Investments that would not be completed until the beginning of the

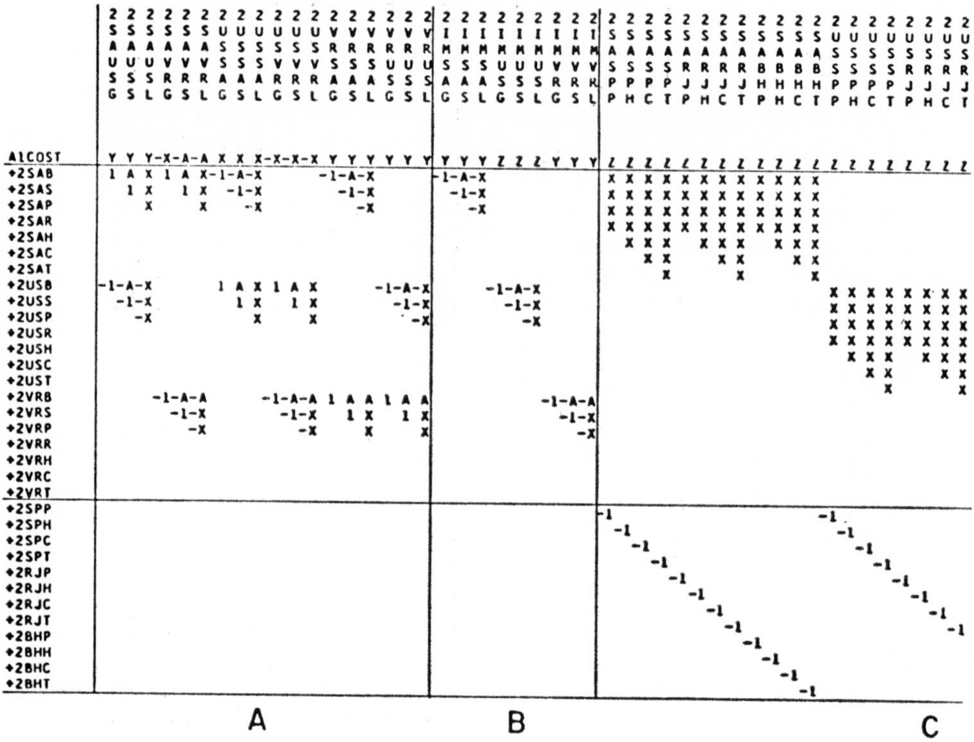
ALCOST
+2SAB
+2SAS
+2SAP
+2SAR
+2SAH
+2SAC
+2SAT
+2USB
+2USS
+2USP
+2USR
+2USH
+2USC
+2UST
+2VRB
+2VRS
+2VRP
+2VRR
+2VRH
+2VRC
+2VRT
+2SPP
+2SPH
+2SPC
+2SPT
+2RJP
+2RJH
+2RJC
+2RJT
+2BHP
+2BHH
+2BHC
+2BHT
A
B
C

FIGURE F.4. *A picture of the*

third or the fourth time period have no effect on the capacity restrictions during the second time period. Therefore, the only entries in this top section of the F matrix are in columns for investment activities of the second time period. The middle part of Figure F.5 shows that projects completed at the beginning of both the second and the third time periods affect the capacity available in the third time period.

An analysis of the RHS column in Figure F.5 shows that the capacity vector $\mathbf{k}$ remains constant over the time periods while the requirements vector $\mathbf{r}_t$ varies with the time period (as determined by the subscript). The capacity vector remains constant unless some of the original (that is, 1965) productive units decrease in capacity due to aging and wear

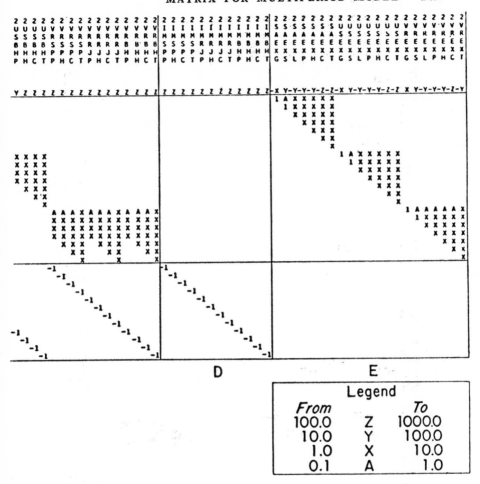

single-period submatrix.

of the equipment or are shut down and removed from the plant. Since two of the plants considered in this model have only been in operation for one or two years and the third plant is not likely to be forced to shut down any of its present production units during the next ten years, it is assumed that none of the major productive units in the existing plants will be removed or will decrease in capacity during the period covered by the model (1967–1975).

The requirements vector r_t changes over time because requirements for steel products in the market areas are expected to increase during the time period covered by the model. In Chapter 6, there is a discussion of the derivation of these market area requirements.

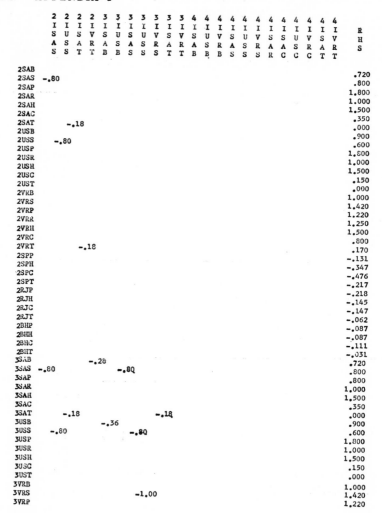

FIGURE F.5. *The investment matrix* F *and the right-hand side.*

The integer constraint submatrix Q and the corresponding right-hand-side vector **h**, which fit beneath the F matrix and the top part of the right-hand side, are shown in Figure F.6.[2] Two additional rows are added to the matrix for each variable that is to be constrained to zero or one (see Figure F.6). The right-hand-side values are then changed as follows to force the variable to take on continuous values (1) be-

[2] This method of constraining a subset of the variables in the model to integer values is outlined by Norman Driebeek in "An Algorithm for the Solution of Mixed Integer Programming Problems," *Management Science,* Vol. 12, No. 7 (March 1966).

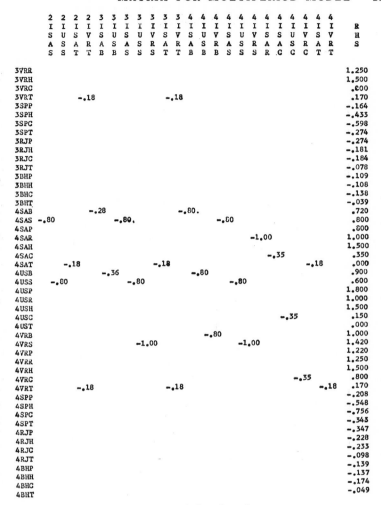

FIGURE F.5 (continued)

tween and including zero and one, (2) exactly at one, or (3) exactly at zero:

2ISAS		Alternative Right-Hand-Side Values		
02ISAS	$1 \leq$	1	1	0
12ISAS	$-1 \leq$	0	-1	0
Value of the variable		$0 \leq 2ISAS \leq 1$	$2ISAS = 1$	$2ISAS = 0$

The advantages of using this system to force the integer variables to take on the values zero or one is the facility with which right-hand sides can be changed in a series of linear programming runs with most linear programming codes.

	2ISAS	2IUSS	2ISAT	2IVRT	3ISAB	3IUSB	3ISAS	3IUSS	3IVRS	3ISAT	3IVRT	4ISAB	4IUSB	4IVRB	4ISAS	4IUSS	4IVRS	4ISAR	4ISAC	4IUSC	4IVRC	4ISAT	4IVRT	RHS
02ISAS	1																							1
12ISAS	-1																							0
02IUSS		1																						1
12IUSS		-1																						0
02ISAT			1																					1
12ISAT			-1																					0
02IVRT				1																				1
12IVRT				-1																				0
03ISAB					1																			1
13ISAB					-1																			0
03IUSB						1																		1
13IUSB						-1																		0
03ISAS							1																	1
13ISAS							-1																	0
03IUSS								1																1
13IUSS								-1																0
03IVRS									1															1
13IVRS									-1															0
03ISAT										1														1
13ISAT										-1														0
03IVRT											1													1
13IVRT											-1													0
04ISAB												1												1
14ISAB												-1												0
04IUSB													1											1
14IUSB													-1											0
04IVRB														1										1
14IVRB														-1										0
04ISAS															1									1
14ISAS															-1									0
04IUSS																1								1
14IUSS																-1								0
04IVRS																	1							1
14IVRS																	-1							0
04ISAR																		1						1
14ISAR																		-1						0
04ISAC																			1					1
14ISAC																			-1					0
04IUSC																				1				1
14IUSC																				-1				0
04IVRC																					1			1
14IVRC																					-1			0
04ISAT																						1		1
14ISAT																						-1		0
04IVRT																							1	1
14IVRT																							-1	0

FIGURE F.6. *The integer constraint submatrix* Q *and the corresponding right-hand side.*

152

Selected Bibliography

Books

Brazil, Government of, Conselho Nacional de Estatistica, *Annuário Estatístico do Brazil,* Rio de Janeiro, 196', 1962, 1963.

Bruno, Michael, *Interdependence, Resource Use and Structural Change in Israel,* Bank of Israel, Jerusalem, 1962.

Comite para la programación de la industria siderúrgica (Committee for the Planning of the Steel Industry), *Programación del desarrollo de la industria de aceros comunes laminador* (The Planning of the Development of the Rolled Steel Products Industry), Nacional Financiera, Mexico, D.F., November 1964.

Gale, D., *The Theory of Linear Economic Models,* McGraw-Hill Book Company, New York, 1960.

Gass, Saul I., *Linear Programming, Methods and Applications,* McGraw-Hill Book Company, New York, 1958.

Hadley, G., *Linear Programming,* Addison-Wesley Publishing Co., Inc., Reading, Mass., 1962.

————, *Non-Linear and Dynamic Programming,* Addison-Wesley Publishing Co., Inc., Reading, Mass., 1964.

Hoover, Edgar M., *The Location of Economic Activity,* McGraw-Hill Book Company, New York, 1948.

Instituto Latinoamericano del Fierro y el Acero (ILAFA, The Latin American Iron and Steel Institute), *Economia siderúrgica latinoamericana-monografías nacionales* (The Latin American Iron and Steel Economy-National Monographs), Casilla 13810, Santiago, Chile, 1963.

Instituto Latinoamericano del Fierro y el Acero (ILAFA), *Repertorio de la empresas siderúrgicas latinoamericanas, 1962–63* (Directory of Latin American Iron and Steel Firms, 1962–63), Casilla 13810, Santiago, Chile, 1962.

Kendrick, David A., "Programming Investment in the Steel Industry," Ph.D. thesis, Department of Economics, Massachusetts Institute of Technology, Cambridge, Mass., 1966.

Lefeber, L., *Allocation in Space,* North-Holland Publishing Company, Amsterdam, Netherlands, 1958.

Manne, A. S., "Investment for Capacity Expansion — Size, Location, and Time Phasing," memo., Stanford University, Stanford, Calif., 1966 (to be published by Allen & Unwin Ltd.).

United Nations, Economic Commission for Europe, *A Comparison of Steel Making Processes,* New York, 1962.

United Nations, Economic Commission for Latin America, "Economía siderúrgica latinoamericana, informe regional," memo., Santiago, Chile, 1964.

United States Steel Corporation, *The Making, Shaping, and Treating of Steel,* Seventh Edition, Pittsburgh, Pa., 1957.

Weingartner, H. Martin, *Mathematical Programming and the Analysis of Capital Budgeting Problems,* Prentice-Hall, Inc., Englewood Cliffs, N.J., 1963.

Articles

Baer, Werner, Isaac Kerstenetzky, and Marios Henrique Simonses, "Transportation and Inflation: A Study of Irrational Policy Making in Brazil," *Economic Development and Cultural Change,* Vol. XIII, No. 2 (January 1965), p. 188.

Chakravarty, Sukhamoy, and R. S. Eckaus, "Choice Elements in Intertemporal Planning Models," in P. M. Rosenstein-Rodan, ed., *Capital Formation and Economic Growth,* Cambridge, Mass., The M.I.T. Press, 1964.

Chakravarty, Sukhamoy, and Louis Lefeber, "An Optimizing Planning Model," *The Economic Weekly,* Annual Number (February 1965), pp. 237–252.

Charnes, A., and W. W. Cooper, "Chance Constrained Programming," *Management Science,* Vol. 6, No. 1 (October 1959), pp. 73–80.

Chenery, Hollis B., "Overcapacity and the Acceleration Principle," *Econometrica,* Vol. 20 (January 1952), pp. 1–28.

———, "The Interdependence of Investment Decisions," in M. Abramovitz, ed., *The Allocation of Economic Resources,* Stanford University Press, Stanford, Calif., 1959.

Cook, S. L., "Applications in the Steel Industry," Chapter 9 in David B. Hertz and Roger T. Eddison, eds., *Progress in Operations Research,* John Wiley & Sons, Inc., New York, 1964, Volume II.

Driebeek, Norman J., "An Algorithm for the Solution of Mixed Integer Programming Problems," *Management Science,* Vol. 12, No. 7 (March 1966), pp. 576–687.

Eckaus, R. S., and L. Lefeber, "Capital Formation: A Theoretical and Empirical Analysis," *Review of Economics and Statistics,* Vol. 44 (May 1962).

Efroymson, M. A., and T. L. Ray, "A Branch and Bound Algorithm for Plant Location," memo., Esso Research and Engineering, 1966.

Hitchcock, R. L., "Distribution of a Product from Several Sources to Numerous Localities," *Journal of Mathematical Physics,* Vol. 20 (1941).

Instituto Latinoamericano del Fierro y el Acero (ILAFA), "Series históricas de consumo aparente, producción, importación y exportación de productos laminados en América Latina, period 1951–62," Santiago, Chile, January 1964.

———, "Estimación del consumo probable de acero laminado para los años 1965, 1970 y 1975," Santiago, Chile, 1964.

Koopmans, T. C., "Optimum Utilization of the Transportation System," *Econometrica,* Vol. 17, Supplement (1949).

Leontief, W. W. "Quantitative Input and Output Relations in the Economic System of the United States," *Review of Economics and Statistics,* Vol. 18 (1936).

Manne, Alan S., "Plant Location Under Economies-of-Scale — Decentralization and Computation," *Management Science,* Vol. 11, No. 2 (November 1964), pp. 213–235.

Markowitz, H. M., and A. S. Manne, "On the Solution of Discrete Programming Problems," *Econometrica,* Vol. 25, No. 1 (January 1957), p. 19 ff.

Martirena-Mantel, Ana María, "Integration and Economies of Scale. The Steel Industry," unpublished paper, Yale University, New Haven, Conn., 1963.

Muller, Gunther H., "Aspectos económicos del proceso Hyl.," Instituto Latinoamericano del Fierro y el Acero, Fourth Latin American Iron and Steel Congress, Mexico City, D.F., 1964.

Reiter, S., and G. R. Sherman, "Discrete Optimizing," mimeo., Purdue University, Lafayette, Ind., February 1963.

Rosenstein-Rodan, Paul N., "Problems of Industrialization of Eastern and Southeastern Europe," in Agarwala, A. N., and S. P. Singh, eds., *The Economics of Underdevelopment,* Oxford University Press, New York, 1963.

Taborga, Pedro N., "Determination of an Optimal System of Transportation for Chile," mimeo., Department of Civil Engineering, Massachusetts Institute of Technology, Cambridge, Mass., January 1965.

TECHINT (Buenos Aires, Argentina) for Propulsora Siderúrgica, "Proyecto de un establecimento siderúrgica a ciclo integral," Milano, Italy, 1964.

United Nations, Interregional Symposium on the Application of Modern Technical Practices in the Iron and Steel Industry to Developing Countries, "The Iron and Steel Industry of Latin America, Plans and Perspectives," Steel Symposium, 1963/Discussion Paper/ECLA. 2, 30 October, 1963.

Vietorisz, Thomas, "Industrial Development Planning Models with Economies of Scale and Indivisibilities," mimeo., IBM Thomas J. Watson Research Center, Yorktown Heights, N.Y., presented at the Third European Congress of the Regional Science Association, August 26–29, 1963, Lund, Sweden.

————, "Locational Choices in Planning," Research Paper RC-1408, IBM Research Center, Yorktown Heights, New York, 1965.

Vietorisz, Thomas, and Alan S. Manne, "Chemical Processes, Plant Location, and Economies of Scale," in Manne, A. S., and H. M. Markowitz, eds., *Studies in Process Analysis* (Cowles Foundation Monograph No. 18), John Wiley & Sons, Inc., New York, 1963, Chapter 6, pp. 136–158.

Weingartner, H. Martin, "On the Capital Budgeting of Interrelated Projects," Report No. 114–65, Alfred P. Sloan School of Management, Massachusetts Institute of Technology, Cambridge, Mass., February 1965.

Periodicals

Blast Furnace and Steel Plant, published monthly by Steel Publications, Inc., Osceola Mills, Pa.

International Financial Statistics, published by the International Monetary Fund, Washington, D.C.

Revista latinoamericana de siderurgia, published monthly by Instituto Latinoamericano del Fierro y el Acero, Santiago, Chile.

Steel, published weekly by The Penton Publishing Company, Cleveland, Ohio.

The New York Times.

The Wall Street Journal.

Index

157